Essentials

of **PSYCHOLOGICAL ASSESSMENT** Series

Everything you need to know to administer, score, and interpret the major psychological tests.

I'd like to order the following
ESSENTIALS OF PSYCHOLOGICAL ASSESSMENT:

All titles are $34.95* each

- ❏ WAIS®-III Assessment / 0471-28295-2
- ❏ WISC-III® and WPPSI-R® Assessment / 0471-34501-6
- ❏ WJ III® Cognitive Abilities Assessment / 0471-34466-4
- ❏ Cross-Battery Assessment / 0471-38264-7
- ❏ Cognitive Assessment with KAIT & Other Kaufman Measures / 0471-38317-1
- ❏ Nonverbal Assessment / 0471-38318-X
- ❏ PAI® Assessment / 0471-08463-8
- ❏ CAS Assessment / 0471-29015-7
- ❏ MMPI-2™ Assessment / 0471-34533-4
- ❏ Myers-Briggs Type Indicator® Assessment / 0471-33239-9
- ❏ Rorschach® Assessment / 0471-33146-5
- ❏ Millon™ Inventories Assessment, Second Edition / 0471-21891-X
- ❏ TAT and Other Storytelling Techniques / 0471-39469-6
- ❏ MMPI-A™ Assessment / 0471-39815-2
- ❏ NEPSY® Assessment / 0471-32690-9
- ❏ Neuropsychological Assessment / 0471-40522-1
- ❏ WJ III® Tests of Achievement Assessment / 0471-33059-0
- ❏ Individual Achievement Assessment / 0471-32432-9
- ❏ WMS®-III Assessment / 0471-38080-6
- ❏ Behavioral Assessment / 0471-35367-1
- ❏ Forensic Assessment / 0471-33186-4
- ❏ Bayley Scales of Infant Development—II Assessment / 0471-32651-8
- ❏ Career Interest Assessment / 0471-35365-5
- ❏ WPPSI™-III Assessment / 0471-28895-0
- ❏ 16PF® Assessment / 0471-23424-9
- ❏ Assessment Report Writing / 0471-39487-4
- ❏ Stanford-Binet Intelligence Scales (SB5) Assessment / 0471-22404-9

Please complete the order form on the back

TO ORDER BY PHONE, CALL TOLL FREE 1-877-762-2974
To order online: www.wiley.com/essentials
To order by mail refer to order form on next page

Essentials

of **PSYCHOLOGICAL ASSESSMENT** Series

Order Form

Please send this order form with your payment (credit card or check) to:

 John Wiley & Sons, Inc.
 Attn: J. Knott
 111 River Street
 Hoboken, NJ 07030

Name _____

Affiliation _____

Address _____

City/State/Zip _____

Phone _____

E-mail _____

❑ Please add me to your e-mailing list

Quantity of Book(s) ordered _____ x $34.95* each

	Surface	2-Day	1-Day	
Shipping charges:				
First Item	$5.00	$10.50	$17.50	
Each additional item	$3.00	$3.00	$4.00	**Total $_____**

For orders greater than 15 items, please contact Customer Care at 1-877-762-2974.

Payment Method: ❑ Check ❑ Credit Card (*All orders subject to credit approval*)
     ❑ MasterCard ❑ Visa ❑ American Express

Card Number _____ Exp. Date_____

Signature _____

           * Prices subject to change.

TO ORDER BY PHONE, CALL TOLL FREE 1-877-762-2974
To order online: www.wiley.com/essentials   **WILEY**

Essentials of Stanford-Binet Intelligence Scales (SB5) Assessment

Essentials of Psychological Assessment Series
Series Editors, Alan S. Kaufman and Nadeen L. Kaufman

Essentials

of Stanford-Binet Intelligence Scales (SB5) Assessment

Gale H. Roid and
R. Andrew Barram

 John Wiley & Sons, Inc.

Published by John Wiley & Sons, Inc., Hoboken, New Jersey.
Published simultaneously in Canada.

Woodcock-Johnson, WJ III, WJ-R, SB5 Scoring Pro and Universal Nonverbal Intelligence Test are registered trademarks of Houghton Mifflin Company.

The Psychological Corporation, WAIS, Wechsler Adult Intelligence Scale, Wechsler Individual Achievement Test, Wechsler Intelligence Scale for Children, WIAT, WISC-III, Wechsler Preschool and Primary Scale of Intelligence, and WPPSI are registered trademarks of The Psychological Corporation.

Millon and MCMI-III are registered trademarks of Pearson Assessments.

DSM-IV is a registered trademark of the American Psychiatric Association.

For general information on our other products and services please contact our Customer Care Department within the United States at (800) 762-2974, outside the United States at (317) 572-3993 or fax (317) 572-4002.

Wiley also publishes its books in a variety of electronic formats. Some content that appears in print may not be available in electronic books. For more information about Wiley products, visit our website at www.wiley.com.

Library of Congress Cataloging-in-Publication Data:

Roid, Gale H.
    Essentials of Stanford-Binet Intelligence Scales (SB5) assessment / Gale H. Roid and R. Andrew Barram.
        p. cm. — (Essentials of psychological assessment series)
    Includes bibliographical references and index.
    ISBN 0-471-22404-9 (pbk.)
        1. Stanford-Binet Test. I. Barram, R. Andrew. II. Title. III. Series.
BF432.5.S8R65 2004
153.9'3—dc22
                                                                                    2004040859

Printed in the United States of America

10 9 8 7 6 5 4 3 2 1

To my family

G. H. R.

To my loving wife and children

R. A. B.

CONTENTS

SERIES PREFACE

In the *Essentials of Psychological Assessment* series, we have attempted to provide the reader with books that will deliver key practical information in the most efficient and accessible style. The series features instruments in a variety of domains, such as cognition, personality, education, and neuropsychology. For the experienced clinician, books in the series will offer a concise yet thorough way to master utilization of the continuously evolving supply of new and revised instruments, as well as a convenient method for keeping up-to-date on the tried-and-true measures. The novice will find here a prioritized assembly of all the information and techniques that must be at one's fingertips to begin the complicated process of individual psychological diagnosis.

Wherever feasible, visual shortcuts to highlight key points are utilized alongside systematic, step-by-step guidelines. Chapters are focused and succinct. Topics are targeted for an easy understanding of the essentials of administration, scoring, interpretation, and clinical application. Theory and research are continually woven into the fabric of each book but always to enhance clinical inference, never to sidetrack or overwhelm. We have long been advocates of what has been called intelligent testing—the notion that a profile of test scores is meaningless unless it is brought to life by the clinical observations and astute detective work of knowledgeable examiners. Test profiles must be used to make a difference in the child's or adult's life, or why bother to test? We want this series to help our readers become the best intelligent testers they can be.

The Stanford-Binet Intelligence Scales, one of the classics of assessment, was recently revised and published in its fifth edition (SB5) (Roid, 2003a). Enhanced features were designed to increase the usefulness of the SB5 for preschool children, individuals with mental retardation, elderly clients with memory difficulties, individuals with intellectual giftedness, and many other applications. The SB5 combines the point scale format of the Fourth Edition (SB4) with the age-level format found in previous editions such as the classic Form L-M. The latest version of the Stanford-Binet is a wide-ranging, individually administered test battery designed for ages 2 through 85+ years; its subtests cover five cognitive factors—Fluid Reasoning, Knowledge (Crystallized ability), Quantitative Reasoning, Visual-Spatial ability, and Working Memory—in both the verbal and nonverbal domains. The SB5 represents a useful addition to the cognitive assessment scene.

Alan S. Kaufman, PhD, and Nadeen L. Kaufman, EdD, Series Editors
Yale University School of Medicine

ACKNOWLEDGMENTS

The authors thank Riverside Publishing, 425 Spring Lake Drive, Itasca, Illinois, 60143, for permission to employ the standardization data and to use various tables and figures from the SB5 test manuals. Researchers should note that permission to use SB5 information should be obtained in writing by contacting Dr. Andrew Carson or the Permissions Department at Riverside Publishing. Importantly, the authors thank their wives and families for patience during the writing of the chapters that follow.

Gale Roid and Andrew Barram
January, 2004

Essentials of Stanford-Binet Intelligence Scales (SB5) Assessment

One

OVERVIEW OF THE SB5 AND ITS HISTORY

INTRODUCTION

New editions of nationally standardized tests provide modern wording, illustrations, enhanced measurement procedures, updated theory and research, and new standardizations, enhancing the validity of test interpretations. Such enhancements come at a price, however, in time, effort, and costs to the developers and consumers. After a 7-year revision project, the Stanford-Binet Intelligence Scale, Fifth Edition (SB5) (Roid, 2003b) was published with enhanced features, norms, and procedures. Initial reviews and receptions by users have shown that the revision project was successful in many respects, to be described in the chapters that follow.

The SB5 combines the point-scale format of the fourth edition (SB4) by Thorndike, Hagen, and Sattler (1986) with the age-level format found in previous editions such as the classic Forms L, M, and L-M (Terman & Merrill, 1937, 1960). Examiners begin a standard test administration by giving the two routing subtests: Object Series/Matrices (nonverbal) and Vocabulary (verbal). Estimates of ability in the nonverbal and verbal domains are obtained from raw scores on each routing test and used to tailor the remaining assessment to the examinee's functional ability. Simple conversion tables show the examiner which functional levels (ranging from easy to hard, Levels 1 through 6) of the nonverbal and verbal scales to continue testing. By adding the nonverbal routing test and an entire one-half of the SB5 in the non-verbal domain, the new edition provides excellent features for testing individuals with limited English or with communication difficulties. The nonverbal section requires a low language demand—that is, minimal receptive language and mostly nonverbal responses (pointing, moving pieces, etc.) by the examinee. Also, the two-stage testing procedure, with routing subtests first and functional-level sections next, provides highly precise estimates of cognitive ability in a relatively short period of time.

Thus, the SB5 is a wide-ranging, individually administered test battery. Norms were designed for ages 2 through 85+ years and the subtests cover five cognitive factors—Fluid Reasoning, Knowledge (crystallized ability), Quantitative Reasoning, Visual-Spatial Processing, and Working Memory—in both the verbal and nonverbal domains. Importantly, the SB5 is the first intellectual battery to cover five cognitive factors in both the nonverbal and verbal domains. Five nonverbal subtests and five verbal subtests measure each of the factors.

Many new features have been added to the SB5 and features of previous editions enhanced, as shown in Rapid Reference 1.1. Many of the new features were designed to enhance the usefulness of the SB5 for assessments with preschool children, individuals with mental retardation, and individuals with intellectual giftedness. In addition, many features were added to make the test easy for examiners to administer and score.

≡ *Rapid Reference 1.1*

New Features of the SB5 Compared to Previous Editions

- Brightly colored toys, blocks, and pictures to enhance preschool assessment.
- New composite scores (IQ and Factor Index) with a mean of 100 and standard deviation of 15, and subtests with a mean of 10 and standard deviation of 3.
- Extended low-end items for early childhood assessment and high-end items for giftedness assessment, including an innovative Extended IQ measuring IQ down to 10 and up to 225.
- An abbreviated IQ based on the two routing subtests.
- Retention of a few classic Binet items such as Picture Absurdities; new scales such as block tapping, recall of the last words in a series of sentences (measuring working memory processes; Baddeley, 1986), and formation of designs using an expanded set of form-board pieces as a replacement for block designs.
- Change-Sensitive Scores, providing criterion-referenced interpretation of scores based on item response theory.
- Linkage to the Woodcock-Johnson III Tests of Achievement for assessment of learning disabilities.
- Interpretation of differences between nonverbal and verbal abilities within each factor to identify strengths and weaknesses in the individual's profile of abilities.

HISTORY

A number of the features of the design of the SB5 become apparent when the history of the Stanford-Binet and its various editions is reviewed. Developments began in France at the turn of the 20th century. Alfred Binet and Theodore Simon (1905) developed a useful tool to assess general intelligence, which is widely cited as the first major breakthrough in intelligence testing. As a member of a French governmental commission working on mental retardation, Binet developed a practical test, sensitive to different levels of cognitive development, that could be given during a clinical interview. Binet's early work is summarized in Rapid Reference 1.2.

Terman's 1916 Stanford Revision

Researchers in the United States, such as Goddard (1908) and Terman (1911), quickly saw the theoretical and practical value of Binet's work and began to adapt the work to the American context. Lewis Terman, of Stanford University, worked with Child (Terman & Child, 1912) to develop a preliminary revision of the Binet-Simon scale. Within a few years, Terman (1916) had extended the scale and collected data on more than 2,300 children and adolescents. The improved scale was published as the *Stanford Revision and Extension of the Binet-Simon Scale* by a division of Houghton-Mifflin Company called Riverside Press. Alternative versions of the Binet-Simon scales that presented intelligence as a singular dimension were distributed in the United States (e.g., the Goddard, 1910 version). However, Terman's 1916 revision retained Binet's concept of intelligence as a complex mixture of abilities, and is the only revision that has stood the test of time, remaining in publication to the present day. The standardization that Terman accomplished was quite rigorous for the early 1900s and increased the scale's technical quality. Also, the scale had thorough directions for examiners and used the ratio of mental age to chronological age first introduced by Stern (1914). This intelligence quotient (IQ) became the new standard for the assessment of intelligence.

Revisions of the Terman Scales in 1937, 1960, and 1972

Within 20 years of its release in 1916, the Stanford Revision emerged as the most widely used test of intellectual ability in America. The scale

≡Rapid Reference 1.2

History of the Early Work of Binet

Alfred Binet (1857–1911) authored almost 300 books, articles, and reviews during his career. His work began with intelligence testing, when Binet collaborated with Victor Henri (1872–1940) to outline a project for the development of a series of mental tasks to measure individual differences (Binet & Henri, 1895). The tasks were designed to differentiate a number of complex mental faculties, including memory, imagery, imagination, attention, comprehension, aesthetic sentiment, moral sentiment, muscular strength, motor ability, and hand-eye coordination.

The 1905 Binet-Simon Scale

Binet was named a member of a government educational commission and took the lead in devising a useful and reliable diagnostic system for identifying children with mental retardation. Binet's project culminated in the publication of the first practical intelligence test (Binet & Simon, 1905) with physician Theodore Simon (1873–1961).

Binet sought to make the 1905 scale efficient and practical: "We have aimed to make all our tests simple, rapid, convenient, precise, heterogeneous, holding the subject in continued contact with the experimenter, and bearing principally upon the faculty of judgment" (from the Kite translation, Binet & Simon, 1916). The scale consisted of 30 items, which were scored on a pass-fail basis. The items presented various word problems, paper-cutting tasks, repeating sentences and digits, and comparing blocks to put them in order by weight (Wolf, 1969). Combinations of mental and physical strategies were required in solving each item or mastering each task. The complex nature of these practical items is generally recognized as the major breakthrough that allowed intelligence to be assessed during a clinical interview. Prior to Binet's use of complex items and tasks, mental abilities were measured in isolated fashion with laboratory equipment and included visual perception, reaction time, hearing acuity, and other physical measurements (e.g., Galton, 1883, as described in Johnson, McClearn, Yuen, Nagoshi, Ahern, & Cole, 1985).

(continued)

The 1905 scale included several important innovations that would be used in subsequent measures of intelligence. Items were ranked in order of difficulty and accompanied by careful instructions for administration. Binet and Simon also utilized the concept of age-graded norms (Wolf, 1973). The use of age-graded items allowed the scale to estimate mental age by the pattern of correct answers.

The 1905 Binet-Simon Scale was revised in 1908 (Binet & Simon, 1908) and again in 1911. By the completion of the 1911 edition, Binet had extended the scales through adulthood and balanced them with five items at each age level. The scales included procedures for assessing language (e.g., receptive naming and expressive naming in response to visual material, repeating sentences, and defining familiar objects), auditory processing (e.g., word rhyming), and visual processing (e.g., rapid discrimination of lines, and drawing the unfolded design of a folded paper with cut portions). Also included were tasks to assess learning and memory (e.g., repeating prose passages, repeating phrases and sentences of increasing length, drawing two designs from memory, recalling the names of pictured objects, and repeating numbers), and judgment and problem solving (e.g., answering problems of social and practical comprehension, giving distinctions between abstract terms).

had several language translations and was used internationally. In subsequent years, Terman continue to experiment with easier and more difficult items to extend the measurement scale downward and upward and to increase the age range by collecting more standardization cases. As was the practice in test publishing at that time, an alternative form of the scale was also developed. Funding came from Stanford University grants and help came from colleague Maud Merrill, who served as codirector of the revision project. Interestingly, the new edition took 7 years to create—the same length of time devoted to the new fifth edition (Roid, 2003f)—and was called the *New Revised Stanford-Binet Tests of Intelligence* (Terman & Merrill, 1937).

The 1937 revision was standardized on 3,200 examinees aged 1 year

6 months to 18 years. Terman made efforts to include a broader representation of geographic regions and socioeconomic levels in the normative sample. Two alternative forms, Form L and Form M, were included. Improvements over the 1916 edition included greater coverage of nonverbal abilities, less emphasis on recall memory, extended range of the scale at the lower and upper ends, and more objectified scoring methods. The descriptions of the norming methods employed on Forms L and M and use of the *Hollerith sorter* (an early data-processing machine that sorted coded punch cards) for statistical analyses are quite impressive and interesting as examples of early psychometric methods (Terman & Merrill, 1937, p. 22).

As happens with any widely used test of ability or achievement, certain items of the 1937 edition became dated by the 1950s, and some of the toys used with the test had become difficult to obtain after World War II. Therefore, Terman and Merrill began a further revision of the scale based on the accumulated information and data collected since 1937. According to the preface in Terman and Merrill (1973, p. vi), "plans for the third revision had been formulated and were well on their way" when Terman died in 1956. Thus, the *Stanford-Binet Intelligence Scale, Third Revision* (Terman & Merrill, 1960) was published. Several new features were included in the third revision (now called the third *edition*), including use of the deviation IQ (standardized normative mean of 100 and standard deviation of 16) rather than the ratio IQ, and production of a combined Form L-M consisting of the most discriminating 142 items from the 1937 forms. Extensive item analyses had been conducted on data from nearly 4,500 subjects from the 1930s to 1950s and any items showing substantial change in difficulty were eliminated or adjusted in sequence. No newly created items were added to Form L-M. Six items were placed at each age level of the combined form (reduced from its previous eight items per level) and some directions were clarified.

After Maud Merrill retired, Robert L. Thorndike of Columbia University was asked to lead a project to collect new norms for the third edi-

DON'T FORGET

History of the Stanford-Binet

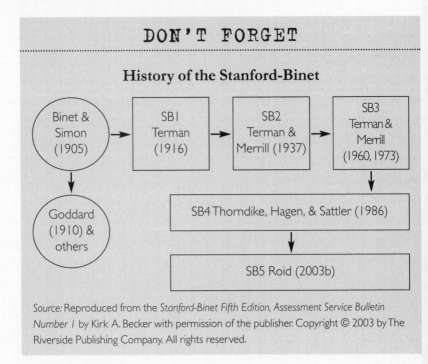

tion. Thus, the same edition was reprinted with the new normative tables—an update of Form L-M (Terman & Merrill, 1973). Because the *Cognitive Abilities Test* (CogAT; Thorndike & Hagen, 1994) was being standardized at the same time as the 1972 renorming of the Stanford-Binet, Thorndike selected subjects and some siblings of subjects tested on the CogAT to compose the new norm sample. The stratification variables used on the sample (e.g., age, geographic region, ethnicity, community size) were similar to those used today, as were the levels of ability on the verbal portion of the CogAT. The items in the test remained essentially the same as on the 1960 revision, with two minor exceptions.

The 1986 Edition by Thorndike, Hagen, and Sattler

With the SB4 (Thorndike et al., 1986), the test took on a new appearance and structure. The SB4 was based on a four-factor, hierarchical model with general ability (*g*) as the overarching summary score. The four cognitive factors were Verbal Reasoning, Abstract/ Visual Reasoning, Quantitative Reasoning, and Short-Term Memory. The most significant change from previous editions, however, was the use of point scales for all subtests rather than the developmental age levels used in previous forms. Vocabulary was still retained as a routing test, allowing the test to be tailored to the examinee's verbal ability. Also, many classic Stan-

> ## CAUTION
>
> As with all published measures of intellectual abilities, the SB5 measures a fixed number (five) of all the multiple dimensions of cognitive abilities and skills that have been researched over the last 100 years. Examiners should be cautious in claiming that all cognitive abilities have been assessed in any one examination or any one test. Also, be cautious in describing the Full Scale IQ as an errorless, fixed entity that summarizes the full potential of the individual.

ford-Binet tasks were retained, including Absurdities, Vocabulary, Matrices, Quantitative Reasoning, and Memory for Sentences—tasks also included in the SB5. Composite scores for each cognitive factor and profile scores for each subtest allowed a comprehensive examination of strengths and weaknesses among abilities within general intelligence.

THEORY AND STRUCTURE OF THE SB5:
THE 2003 FIFTH EDITION

Based on the important research of Carroll (1993), the SB5 was constructed on a five-factor hierarchical cognitive model. The five factors were derived from the combined models of Carroll, Cattell (1943), and Horn (1965). The combination of models, now called the Cattell-Horn-Carroll (CHC) theory, normally lists 8 to 10 factors. Many of the supplemental factors, such as processing speed, auditory processing, and long-term retrieval, require specialized timing or test apparatus (e.g.,

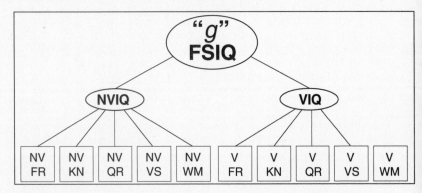

Figure 1.1 The Hierarchical Structure of the SB5 Scoring System

Notes: FSIQ = Full Scale IQ; *g* = general ability; NVIQ = Nonverbal IQ; VIQ = Verbal IQ; FR = Fluid Reasoning; KN = Knowledge; QR = Quantitative Reasoning; VS = Visual-Spatial Processing; WM = Working Memory.

tape recorders). However, the five cognitive factors of the SB5 (see Fig. 1.1) were selected based on research on school achievement and on expert ratings of the importance of these factors in the assessment of reasoning, especially in giftedness assessment. Also, the memory factor was shifted from an emphasis on short-term memory only, as in the fourth edition of the Stanford-Binet, to an emphasis on Working Memory. Therefore, the overall model shown in Figure 1.1 is a hierarchical *g* model with five factors emphasizing reasoning abilities that can be easily administered within a one-hour assessment. The important change in emphasis in the fifth edition is the duplication of all five cognitive factors in both the nonverbal and verbal domains.

The structure of the SB5 is also shown in Figure 1.1. The verbal and nonverbal domains include five subtests each, for a total of 10 profile scores. The nonverbal subtests require a small degree of receptive language and allow for pointing responses, the movement of puzzle-like pieces, and manipulation of toys to indicate correct answers. The verbal subtests require facility with words and printed material (reading or speaking). A description of each of the 10 subtests is provided in Rapid Reference 1.3.

Subtests of the SB5

Subtest	Description (activities at various levels)
Nonverbal	
Fluid Reasoning	Object Series/Matrices (a point scale used for routing). Includes new sequential reasoning items and classic matrices.
Knowledge	Procedural Knowledge (a new type of item involving gestures), followed by Picture Absurdities (a classic subtest in the Stanford-Binet tradition).
Quantitative Reasoning	Nonverbal Quantitative Reasoning items, tapping number concepts, problem solving, and figural-geometric/ measurement-estimation problems.
Visual-Spatial Reasoning	Form Board (classic items for the lower levels), followed by the new Form Patterns (making designs from an expanded set of form-board pieces).
Working Memory	Delayed Response (e.g., hiding an object under a cup) at the low levels followed by Block Span (the new block-tapping procedure).
Verbal	
Fluid Reasoning	Early Reasoning items (e.g., picture reasoning) followed by classic Verbal Absurdities and Verbal Analogies.
Knowledge	Vocabulary (a point scale used for routing). Includes toys, identification of body parts, Child Card, and classic word definitions.
Quantitative Reasoning	Verbal Quantitative Reasoning items, tapping number concepts, problem solving, and figural-geometric/measurement-estimation problems.
Visual-Spatial Reasoning	Innovative new Position and Direction (verbal-spatial problems requiring explanation of directions, identifying spatial relations in pictures, understanding complex statements of spatial orientation).
Working Memory	Classic Memory for Sentences followed by an innovative Last Word procedure (requiring memory of the last word of series of questions).

Psychometric Properties

Extensive studies of reliability, validity, and fairness were conducted as part of the SB5 standardization. The SB5's main technical features are briefly outlined here. The normative sample for the SB5 included 4,800 subjects aged 2 to 96 years. The highest age grouping employed in the norm tables was 85+. The composition of the normative sample closely approximated the stratification percentages reported by the U.S. Census Bureau (2001). Stratification variables included gender, geographic region, ethnicity (African-, Asian-, and Anglo/Caucasian-American; Hispanic; Native American; and Other), and socioeconomic level (years of education completed, or parent's educational attainment). Additionally, subjects were tested ($N = 1,365$) from officially documented special groups such as individuals with mental retardation, learning disabilities, attention deficit, and speech or hearing impairments.

Internal-consistency reliability ranged from .95 to .98 for IQ scores and from .90 to .92 for the five Factor Index scores. For the 10 subtests, average reliabilities (across age groups) ranged from .84 to .89, providing a strong basis for profile interpretation (see Rapid Reference 1.4). Split-half reliability formulas were used for subtests and composite reliabilities for IQ and Factor Index scores.

Test-retest and interexaminer reliability studies were also conducted and showed the stability and consistency of SB5 scoring.

Evidence for content-, criterion-, and construct-related validity of the SB5 was detailed in Roid (2003f), including extensive studies of concurrent, predictive, and factorial validity. Also, good evidence of consequential validity and fairness of predicting achievement were reported in Roid (2003d). Examples of validity, including the correlations with other assessment batteries, are shown in Rapid Reference 1.5. The correlations shown are quite substantial and similar in magnitude to the concurrent correlations observed for other major intelligence batteries.

≡ Rapid Reference 1.4

Average Reliability of SB5 Scores

	Split-Half Reliability	Standard Error of Measurement
Full Scale IQ	.98	2.30
Nonverbal IQ	.95	3.26
Verbal IQ	.96	3.05
Abbreviated IQ	.91	4.55
Favorite Index Scores		
Fluid Reasoning	.90	4.85
Knowledge	.92	4.36
Quantitative Reasoning	.92	4.33
Visual-Spatial Processing	.92	4.41
Working Memory	.92	4.62
Nonverbal Subtests		
Fluid Reasoning	.86	1.18
Knowledge	.85	1.18
Quantitative Reasoning	.86	1.14
Visual-Spatial Processing	.87	1.12
Working Memory	.88	1.07
Verbal Subtests		
Fluid Reasoning	.86	1.18
Knowledge	.89	1.01
Quantitative Reasoning	.87	1.09
Visual-Spatial Processing	.88	1.07
Working Memory	.84	1.22

Source: Roid (2003f).

Rapid Reference 1.5

Correlations of SB5 Full Scale IQ (FSIQ) With Other Tests

Test	Correlation	N
Stanford-Binet Intelligence Scale, Fourth Edition (SB4), Composite	.90	104
Stanford-Binet Form L-M, IQ	.85	80
Wechsler Intelligence Scale for Children–Third Edition (WISC-III), FSIQ	.84	66
Wechsler Adult Intelligence Scale–Third Edition (WAIS-III), FSIQ	.82	87
Wechsler Preschool and Primary Scale of Intelligence–Revised (WPPSI-R), FSIQ	.83	71
Woodcock-Johnson III Tests of Cognitive Abilities, five factors	.90	145
Woodcock-Johnson III Tests of Achievement		
Broad Reading Skills	.66	472
Broad Math	.76	472
Wechsler Individual Achievement Test–Second Edition		
Reading	.67	80
Mathematics	.79	80

Source: Reproduced from the *Stanford-Binet Fifth Edition, Technical Manual* by Gale H. Roid, Ph.D., with permission of the publisher. Copyright © 2003 by The Riverside Publishing Company. All rights reserved.

The substantial predictive correlations between the SB5 and two major achievement batteries—the Woodcock-Johnson III (WJ III) and the Wechsler Individual Achievement Test–Second Edition (WIAT-II)—provide a strong basis for comparing intellectual and achievement scores of individuals.

Extensive studies of the factor structure of the SB5 were conducted, including confirmatory factor analyses using LISREL 8.3 (Joreskog & Sorbom, 1999). The factor analyses were calculated for five successive age groups (2–5, 6–10, 11–16, 17–50, and 51+) comparing factor models with one, two, three, four, and five factors. Split-half scores (scores for odd- and even-numbered items in each of the 10 subtests) were employed to provide more stable estimates of each factor in the maximum-likelihood analyses. The five-factor models showed superior fit, including the non-normed fit index (NNFI), ranging from .89 to .93; the comparative fit index (CFI), ranging from .91 to .93; and the root mean square error of approximation (RMSEA), ranging from .076 to .088. A second series of confirmatory analyses was conducted with LISREL using conventional full-length subtests across two batteries: the SB5 and the WJ III (Woodcock, McGrew, & Mather, 2001b). Again, the five-factor model showed the best fit, with alignment of the fluid, knowledge, quantitative, visual, and memory factors across the SB5 and WJ III as predicted.

COMPREHENSIVE REFERENCES ON THE TEST

Ethical guidelines and details of test administration, scoring, and interpretation of the SB5 are covered in the *Examiner's Manual* (Roid, 2003c). Details of the development and standardization; characteristics of the normative sample; and extensive studies of reliability, fairness, and validity are presented in the *Technical Manual* (Roid, 2003f). Additional statistical analyses, useful tables, and case studies are presented in the *Interpretive Manual* (Roid, 2003d) and in Roid and Pomplun (in press). Rapid Reference 1.6 provides basic information about the SB5 and its publisher.

≡Rapid Reference 1.6

Description of Stanford-Binet Intelligence Scale, Fifth Edition (SB5)

Author: Gale H. Roid

Publication Date: 2003

What the test measures: Nonverbal, verbal, and general intellectual abilities

Age Range: 2 to 85+ years

Administration Time: Entire battery 45 to 75 min, depending on the examinee. Nonverbal or verbal sections separately, 30 min each. Abbreviated battery (two subtests), 15–20 min.

Qualification of Examiners: Graduate or professional-level training in psychological assessment.

Publisher: Riverside Publishing
420 Spring Lake Drive
Itasca, IL 60143
(800) 767-8420

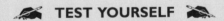 **TEST YOURSELF**

1. **How many routing subtests are there on the SB5, and what are their names?**

   (a) One—Vocabulary

   (b) One—Object Series/Matrices

   (c) Two—Vocabulary and Nonverbal Visual-Spatial

   (d) Two—Vocabulary and Object Series/Matrices

2. **What is the main advantage of the two-stage testing in the SB5 (routing subtests followed by functional levels)?**

   (a) Reduced emphasis on speed of response

   (b) Greater measurement precision in a shorter time

   (c) Higher predictive validity

   (d) Ease of test administration for the examiner

3. **Name the author(s) and the publication date of the first version of the Stanford-Binet published in America.**

   (a) Binet & Henri, 1895

   (b) Stern, 1910

   (c) Terman, 1916

   (d) Terman & Merrill, 1937

4. **Which edition of the Stanford-Binet replaced the original intelligence quotient (ratio IQ) with the deviation IQ?**

   (a) Second, 1937

   (b) Third, 1960

   (c) Fourth, 1986

   (d) Fifth, 2003

5. **How many cognitive factors, domains, and subtests does the SB5 contain?**

   (a) Four factors; one general domain; 8 subtests

   (b) Four factors; quantitative and verbal domains; 12 subtests

   (c) Five factors; nonverbal and verbal domains; 8 subtests

   (d) Five factors; nonverbal and verbal domains; 10 subtests

6. **What is the range of subtest average reliability (split-half) on the SB5?**

   (a) .74 to .79

   (b) .84 to .89

   (c) .90 to .92

   (d) .95 to .98

7. **What are the age range and approximate administration time of the full-battery SB5?**

   (a) 2 to 21 years, 30 to 45 min

   (b) 6 to 16 years, 50 to 75 min

   (c) 18 to 74 years, 60 min

   (d) 2 to 85+ years, 45 to 75 min

(continued)

8. **Which edition of the Stanford-Binet introduced a cognitive model with hierarchical g and four primary cognitive factors?**

   (a) Second, 1937

   (b) Third, 1960

   (c) Fourth, 1986

   (d) Fifth, 2003

9. **What was the size of the normative sample of the SB5 and the age of the oldest subject tested?**

   (a) 4,800, 96 years

   (b) 3,560, 85 years

   (c) 2,200, 74 years

   (d) 1,365, 69 years

10. **Which is an example of a classic type of Stanford-Binet item that was retained in the fifth edition?**

    (a) Picture Absurdities

    (b) Form Patterns

    (c) Last Word

    (d) Block Span

Answers: 1. d; 2. b; 3. c; 4. b; 5. d; 6. b; 7. d; 8. c; 9. a; 10. a

Two

HOW TO ADMINISTER THE SB5

The author and test developers of the SB5 designed the edition with examiners in mind, making it easy to administer (Roid, 2003f). Examiner directions for each item of the scales are printed on the examiner pages of the *item books*—the easels used to administer the SB5. The SB5 *record form* is designed in a format familiar to psychologists and other professionals who have used other intelligence batteries. A plastic tray for toys and manipulable pieces ("manipulatives") is provided in the SB5 kit to facilitate the flow of materials during testing. All of these features were field tested over a 7-year period of test development, with feedback from examiners.

This chapter presents guidelines and suggestions for planning and conducting effective test administrations with the SB5. General testing considerations such as standardization, definitions, physical arrangements, and building rapport are discussed along with preparations for testing. Finally, more details of administration for each subtest, along with examiner tips, are provided.

GENERAL TESTING CONSIDERATIONS

The most important consideration in testing with the SB5 is to follow the standardized directions exactly. For ease of use, the directions are printed clearly on the examiner's pages of the three item books, and further suggestions and tips for examiners are presented in the *Examiner's*

Manual. If the examinee has significant disabilities that make the standard response methods (pointing, moving blocks, etc.) difficult, accommodations may be required. (See Braden & Elliott, 2003; Roid, 2003c, 2003d. Also see the brief discussion of accommodations in the section on Testing Individuals with Special Needs, later in this chapter.)

Definitions of important terminology will help you understand the structure and administration of the SB5. Rapid Reference 2.1 provides brief definitions of key terms used in SB5 administration: items, testlets, subtests, functional levels, factors, domains, and composite scores. The SB5 introduced the term *testlet* to describe a brief set of three to six items that are placed within each of the functional levels of Item Book 2 (the nonverbal levels) and Item Book 3 (the verbal levels). *Testlets* is a term attributed to Wainer (1990) and has been studied extensively in achievement testing programs and scholastic aptitude tests. Testing begins with the routing subtests in Item Book 1 and continues on in Item Book 2 and then Item Book 3, in the standard order of administration.

Physical arrangements for testing should include a relatively noise-free environment with a table and chairs of appropriate size for the examinee and examiner. As is common in individual test administration, the examinee sits either across the table from the examinee (if all examinee responses can be seen over the easel item books) or at a 90-deg angle from the examinee at the side of the table. The examiner should post a "testing in session" sign on the door of the room if there is any chance of interruptions during the testing. Any unusual interruptions of testing, unexpectedly loud noises, or other distractions should be noted in the behavioral observation notes of the examiner. The examiner should use a clipboard or other method of keeping the record form out of sight of the examinee because the form contains some pictures that might cue responses. Also, for the SB5, it is recommended that all the manipulative pieces (blocks, toys, chips, counting rods, etc.) be arranged in the plastic tray provided, in an order chosen by the exam-

≡Rapid Reference 2.1

Definitions of Terms Used in SB5 Assessment

- *Items:* The questions or individual tasks throughout the test.
- *Testlets:* Short tests consisting of three to six items (or any task producing about 6 points), arrayed in levels of increasing difficulty.
- *Subtests:* Either the routing subtests or the sum of all the testlet scores added together to form subtest factor scores. Routing subtests function to estimate the ability of the examinee so that the remaining portion of the test can be tailored to the ability level of the examinee. Normative subtest scores are called *scaled scores* and range from 1 to 19 with a mean of 10 and standard deviation of 3.
- *Functional levels:* Within Item Books 2 and 3, items are organized into testlets of increasing difficulty. Each level has four testlets; nonverbal testlets have six levels (Levels 1 to 6) and verbal testlets have five levels (labeled Levels 2 to 6).
- *Factors:* The five cognitive abilities measured by the SB5—Fluid Reasoning, Knowledge, Quantitative Reasoning, Visual-Spatial Processing, and Working Memory. Each factor is measured by testlets within Item Books 2 and 3 (and with scoring records located in each of the four corners of the record form), or by one of the two routing subtests in Item Book 1.
- *Domains:* Two major parts of the SB5—the nonverbal (Item Book 2) or nonverbal (Item Book 3)—representing two modes of responding to SB5 items.
- *Composite scores:* Either IQ scores (Full Scale, Nonverbal, Verbal, and Abbreviated) or Factor Index scores (five of them), all measured on scales with a mean of 100 and standard deviation of 15.

iner. The plastic tray should be placed on a side chair or other location out of sight of small children to prevent distractions by the attractive toys. If the child shows great interest in the toys, it is wise to have alternative toys available at the start and end of testing to prevent the child from attempting to hold and keep the test materials.

Building and Maintaining Rapport

The establishment of rapport is critical in effective administration of psychological tests. This is particularly true with intelligence testing, which demands sustained effort and attention from both the examinee and the examiner. The final scores should represent an examinee's best effort, most easily accomplished when he or she engages in the task. Experienced examiners understand that examinees may arrive with marked anxiety, distractibility, poor motivation, and other conditions that detract from the ideal quality of participation. An examinee may be markedly anxious due to past testing experiences, a history of struggles in school, general low self-esteem, or concerns about the final outcome of the testing (as in forensic testing situations). The examiner should discover these issues before beginning the test and attempt to ameliorate any counterproductive examinee attitudes.

The first part of establishing rapport is to consider the examinee's concerns regarding testing. An examinee may be willing to discuss such concerns in advance of initiating the testing. Before beginning, the examiner should explain the process of the test in a manner that elicits comments from the examinee to highlight any concerns. The examiner should address these concerns in a manner that the examinee can understand. After this discussion, wait until the examinee clearly indicates a readiness to begin testing. When testing very young children it is important to make sure the child sees that the parent or caregiver is comfortable with the evaluation procedures.

The administration directions in the item books provide instructions for introducing each task within the SB5. The examiner's familiarity with administering the SB5 will facilitate proceeding at a pace that is comfortable for the examinee. If comfortable with administration tasks, an examiner can monitor the experience of the examinee and adjust the pace or administration style as necessary to further facilitate rapport. A too-slow pace may increase boredom and thereby decrease effort. A pace that is too rapid may lead an examinee to feel rushed and perhaps frustrated. Tasks should be presented rapidly enough to maintain examinee interest without being overwhelming. The examiner should find the most comfortable pace for the examinee.

Rapport should be maintained throughout the administration while following the standardized protocol. The standardized administration allows the examiner to be relaxed and personable, while maintaining professionalism. The more familiar you are with the SB5, the more focused you can be in dealing with the examinee. The SB5 was designed to ensure that the subtests would be enjoyable and engaging for most examinees. Maintaining rapport throughout the administration may include taking unplanned breaks for the examinee. Small conversations or friendly comments may be helpful between testlets. Maintaining rapport is important, but examiners are advised to temper their encouragement of the examinee. Do not fall prey to the desire to encourage examinees by telling them when they are correct or incorrect. This may be appreciated by examinees, but falls outside the realm of standardized administrations and amounts to coaching. However, comments such as "Good effort" and "I'm impressed by how hard you are trying" would be appropriate. A positive testing experience for the examinee should result in better measurement.

Testing Individuals With Special Needs

General Considerations

By *special needs,* we usually mean documented, officially designated clinical diagnoses or special education placements. However, examiners well know that many undiagnosed cases exist and examinees do appear with highly emotional, distracted, or even bizarre behaviors that emerge during testing. Generally, the examiner must show sensitivity, patience, willingness to extend the rapport-building stage, and extra effort to obtain eye contact or focused attention with such examinees.

DON'T FORGET

....

When preparing to administer the SB5 to an examinee with known disabilities, linguistic challenges, or significant cultural differences, review the information regarding accommodations in administration. Acceptable accommodations include altering the response or presentation format (e.g., allowing sign language), the amount of time between tests, and the test setting. When accommodations are indicated, follow the recommendations where possible. Review this information in advance so that the administration can be smooth rather than disjointed.

Once you are intimately familiar with the SB5, it may be possible to use some of the materials (those normally used for tasks far below the examinee's ability or those used for extremely advanced tasks) to establish connection with the examinee and engage him or her in the testing session. Talking to caregivers prior to the examination may uncover possible rewards or techniques useful for reinforcing the examinee's engagement in testing. In extreme cases, the test may have to be divided into sections (e.g., routing subtests, nonverbal book, verbal book) and given on separate occasions. When these various techniques are effective in giving a valid test session, the standard SB5 test-administration methods can be employed, allowing for valid use of the normative comparisons of scores. For severe disabilities, consider using accommodations to the standard test administration methods (see Accommodations in Test Administration). When modifications are made that go beyond the typical accommodations, however, the use of normative scoring may be in question because the SB5 standardization was based on standard test-administration procedures. Alternative scoring procedures that do not require comparison to age-group peers are available with the SB5; these are discussed in Chapter 3.

Accommodations in Test Administration

Some examinees will have a legal right to accommodations of the test-administration methods, whether by an extension of time or changes in the allowable methods of responding. Also, ethical guidelines of practice (e.g., American Psychological Association [APA], 2002) require professionals to respond to the unique needs of the client. Finally, the validity of the test will often depend on the proper engagement of the examinee with the test materials and the use of valid presentation and response modes for the atypical examinee (Braden & Elliott, 2003). There is a distinction between a proper test accommodation and test modifications (Thurlow, Elliott, & Ysseldyke, 1998). With *accommodations,* the basic construct validity of the SB5 will be retained because the targeted cognitive skills (e.g., fluid reasoning, working memory) remain intact. Test *modifications* are those procedures that alter the cognitive requirements of a test such as the SB5 (e.g., using easier items; making tasks into measures of attention rather than reasoning; providing clues to correct responses). Rapid Reference 2.2 shows the six general methods of providing valid test accommodations.

Some simple alterations to the typical administration format will provide beneficial accommodations. When concerned about an examinee's starting with items that may seem too difficult, the examiner can elect to choose an earlier start point for a particular subtest. This can be especially effective in providing examinees with some perceptions of initial success. Preschool-age children and individuals with significant disabilities may especially appreciate an administration style that emphasizes a game-like format of testlets. The examiner may also reference the game titles or activity names to increase engagement in the task. Eliminating the verbal domain can be appropriate for administration of the SB5 to individuals whose dominant language is not English, who have significant speech production or auditory reception disabilities, or who are diagnosed with autism. More-specialized accommodations are explained within the *Examiner's Manual* (Roid, 2003c). Examiners who encounter testing situations necessitating special accommodations should review the manual for a more detailed presentation of specialized accommodations that still retain appropriate administration guidelines.

≡Rapid Reference 2.2

Six General Methods of Test Accommodation

- *Presentation format.* Using sign language or other communication methods for deafness or hard-of-hearing conditions; Braille versions of verbal items; allowing magnification for visual impairments; allowing repetition of items that are not repeated in standard administration.
- *Response format.* Allowing examinees to gesture or point rather than use expressive language; allowing technological response devices or hand-writing of verbal responses; assisting with hand movements and responses of individuals with severe orthopedic impairments or paralysis.
- *Timing.* Modifying time limits, durations, lengths of testing sessions, or intervals for items and subtests.
- *Selecting portions of the test.* Using only the nonverbal sections for non–English speakers; using only the verbal sections for visually challenged individuals; selecting certain tasks for children with severe autism.
- *Changing the physical test setting.* Using special equipment for individuals in wheel chairs, hospital beds, and so on.
- *Alternative tests or methods.* Substituting additional nonverbal tests in combination with selected portions of the SB5; testing the limits by repeating memory items or creating multiple-choice versions of free-response items; using dynamic test-teach-test paradigms.

Source: Technical standards published by the committee on test standards composed of members from the American Educational Research Association, American Psychological Association, and National Council on Measurement in Education (1999).

When considering accommodations, examiners should be aware of the distinction between access skills and target skills (Braden & Elliott, 2003). *Access skills* of an examinee include attending, listening, seeing, sitting still, reading, tracking movements, and following directions. *Target skills* for the SB5 include the cognitive abilities of reasoning, knowing, quantifying, visualizing, and remembering—the cognitive factors assessed by the SB5. The accommodations listed in Rapid Reference 2.2 are intended to maintain the requirements of the target skills while changing only the access skills.

USING THE RECORD FORM AND ITEM BOOKS

All the procedures, scoring guides, and spoken examiner prompts are printed on the examiner pages of the item books. Examiners can easily learn the test by opening the kit to the first page of Item Book 1 and following the printed directions. The record form also provides reminders of start and stop rules, scoring methods for each subtest or testlet, procedures for routing, and basal and ceiling rules. The standard order of administration is shown in Figure 2.1. The record form and the sequence of item books (from Item Book 1 to Item Book 3) are designed in this standard order of administration to facilitate testing. Thus, examiners begin with page 3 of the record form (the first routing subtest) and proceed through the routing subtests. After scoring the routing subtests, take the total raw scores to the routing tables located on page 5 (verbal) or page 6 (nonverbal) of the record form.

Remember that the routing procedure is designed to tailor the test to the examinee's level of ability. This adaptive method will give you a more precise assessment of ability in a shorter period of time. Thus, the extra effort to learn and understand the simple routing procedures is well invested. Then turn to the levels indicated by the tables, first to the starting level in Item Book 2 (nonverbal) and then to the starting level in Item Book 3 (verbal). Each level of the item books is coded by a colored stripe along the bottom of each page to facilitate finding the beginning of each level.

Mark scores on the record form during testing so that start, stop, basal, and ceiling rules can be properly evaluated. Mark scores according to the following general types of examinee responses:

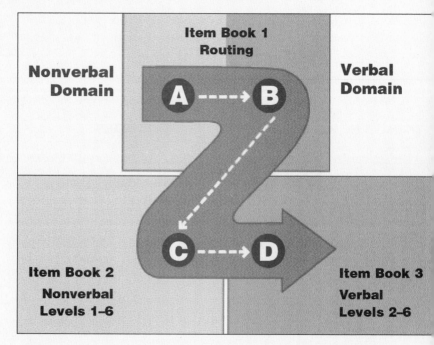

Figure 2.1 Standard Administration Order for the SB5 Item Books

Source: Roid (2003c). Reproduced from the *Stanford-Binet Fifth Edition, Examiner's Manual* by Gale H. Roid, Ph.D., with permission of the publisher. Copyright © 2003 by The Riverside Publishing Company. All rights reserved.

1. For multiple-choice-type items, circle either the letter of the correct answer (e.g., on Object Series/Matrices) or simply the 0 (incorrect) or 1 (correct) item scores for most of the testlets in the item books.

2. For constructed responses such as those to Vocabulary, Picture and Verbal Absurdities, Verbal Analogies, or Early Reasoning, write a verbatim version of the examinee's response in the space provided, and then circle the score (0, 1, or 2) for each item.

3. Circle the score of 0, 1, or 2 by applying the scoring rules shown on the examiner pages of the item books for two of

DON'T FORGET
....

Starting and Stopping Rules for the Routing Subtests

- Note that the rules for starting and stopping are different on the routing subtests of Item Book 1, as compared to the functional levels in Item Books 2 and 3.

- Start testing at the estimated ability level of the examinee (estimated from either chronological age or age and background). Use the record form where the start points are printed as colored headers at certain items. For Fluid Reasoning (page 3 of the record form), start points are located at Items 1, 5, 14 and 18.

- Use the *reverse rule* (dropping back to the next lowest start point) if the examinee fails to respond correctly to either of the first two items at your initial starting point.

- Use the *stop rule* of four consecutive zero scores to discontinue testing.

the levels subtests: (a) Verbal Working Memory (Memory for Sentences or Last Word) and (b) Nonverbal Visual-Spatial Processing (Form Patterns).

SPECIFIC ADMINISTRATION DIRECTIONS FOR SUBTESTS AND TESTLETS

Most of the items in the SB5 are simple for examiners to present and score. Detailed directions, including the exact wording of examiner's spoken prompts, are printed on the examiner direction pages of the item books. Most of the items are objectively scored with multiple-choice or easy dichotomous (0-1) scoring. A few of the SB5 subtests require some practice and are a bit more complex because they are designed to measure clinically meaningful testing behaviors and allow for partially correct responses (scores of 0, 1, or 2). Any tasks requiring additional practice by the examiner are highlighted in the directions that follow.

The Routing Subtests

Nonverbal Fluid Reasoning

Object Series/Matrices is the first subtest in Item Book 1 and the first subtest administered in the standard order of test administration. Begin at the estimated ability level of the examinee (usually the chronological age of the person) at the start point designated on the record form, page 3. Use the Layout Card and colored plastic shapes for the first eight items (usually for children between 2 and 6 years of age). Arrange the plastic pieces, toys, blocks, and so forth in the plastic tray provided with the kit. The order of pieces is not critical—whatever arrangement is convenient for you as the examiner. Place the tray on a side chair out of sight and reach of young children, but within your reach, so that pieces can be easily accessed and returned to the tray.

Take time to carefully teach the starting-point items (Item 1 and Item 5) by following all directions printed in Item Book 1. On Item 4, it is a good idea to find and separate out, in advance, the blue sorting chip with a picture of the basketball and have it ready for use. On Item 7, the red counting rod with six sections is made from 3 of the two-unit rods. Follow the directions on Item 9 to teach the concept of a matrix. Use gestures and pointing to emphasize the location of the piece that is missing (point to

DON'T FORGET

....

Allow sufficient time to carefully calculate the final scores in the two routing testlets. Miscalculations can lead to starting the examinee at an inappropriate level, possibly increasing her or his anxiety or fatigue and certainly jeopardizing rapport. Take a brief break to make sure that the administration moves accurately from the routing procedure into the remainder of the SB5.

the box on the examinee's page with the question mark in it), across the top row (smaller yellow triangle changing to larger red triangle), across the bottom two boxes, and, finally, across all the response options at the bottom of the page. Similar teaching items appear at the start points located at Item 14 and Item 18.

The subtest has a maximum of 36 items, but you would not be expected to administer all items. Be sure that you count the *base points* (see notes in the shaded lines on the record form directly below each start point—refer to Fig. 2.2) to give credit for the easier items located below the starting point for your examinee. Without the base points, the normative comparison of scores would be invalid.

Nearly all SB5 items are untimed to prevent speed from being mixed

Score Routing Tests

1. **Find and circle the Base Points value**
   (located in Record Form below Start Point used).

   > **Start Point Age 5 to 6**
   >
   > **Base Points for start here:** (**4**)

2. **Count and sum the number of points the examinee earned.**

3. **Enter the Base Points and Earned Points. Total to obtain raw score.**

| Base Points | **4** | + | Earned Points | **9** | = | Raw Score: Object Series/Matrices | **13** |

Figure 2.2 Scoring Method for Routing Subtests

into the general ability score. However, for the most difficult items in Matrices (Items 19 to 36), an examiner prompt is allowed to prevent the testing session from getting too long and frustrating the examinee. Some examinees may be shy or embarrassed to admit that they are unable to solve the difficult Matrices items and simply delay in responding. Experienced clinicians watch carefully for signs of frustration, quiet resignation, distraction, fatigue, or a general feeling of giving up. Studies of examinees in the standardization of the SB5 showed that only rarely did response times exceed 2 min. The prompt rule (printed on the examiner pages of Item Book 1), therefore, is to say "Shall we try another one?" after 2 min from the introduction of the item, and then to say "Let's move on to the next one" after an additional minute. Clearly, if all 293 items of the SB5 took 3 min each, testing would last nearly 1½ days! Thus, some type of practical limit must be employed for difficult items in Matrices and also in Quantitative Reasoning (both nonverbal and verbal, Levels 5 and 6).

Verbal Knowledge

Vocabulary is the second routing test in the SB5. Use starting points based on estimated ability or age, as with Object Series/Matrices. The easiest items begin with the identification of facial features, followed by identification of features on the separate Child Card. Use the *boy* side for males and the *girl* side for females, for maximum identification by the examinee. By Item 6, toys are used for identification, followed by a series of picture vocabulary items, until Item 15 and all other items focus on definitions of words. The record form has spaces for recording the exact words of the examinee's definitions. Items 15 to 44 allow scoring of superior (2-point), limited (1-point), and poor (0-point) responses. Examples for each scoring category are provided on the examiner pages of Item Book 1, Verbal Routing section. The scoring examples were collected from real responses of the standardization sample, and represent the most common responses in each category. Additional examples are given in the SB5 *Examiner's Manual*.

CAUTION

Common Pitfalls and Examiner Tips for Administration of the Routing Subtests

Nonverbal Fluid Reasoning: Object Series/Matrices

- Remember that the reverse rule sends you back to the previous start point, not the previous item.
- The examinee may point to the answer option without speaking.
- For difficult items, use the examiner-prompt timing rule (maximum of 3 min).
- An explanation of the logic of the difficult answers is provided in the *Examiner's Manual*.

Verbal Knowledge: Vocabulary

- When responses are unclear or vague, and a *Q* appears in the answer-key section of the examiner directions in Item Book 1, say "Tell me more" to clarify the answer.
- Pronunciation notations are included on the examiner direction pages in Item Book 1. Note that Item 37 has two equally correct pronunciations.
- For examinees at ages 10 and above with a dominant language other than English, or in cases of mental retardation or severe communication disorder, it may be wise to start the examinee at Item 10, using the pictures, instead of the standard Item 15 where the word definitions begin. This could prevent early frustration.

Source: Reproduced from the *Stanford-Binet Fifth Edition, Examiner's Manual* by Gale H. Roid, Ph.D., with permission of the publisher. Copyright © 2003 by The Riverside Publishing Company. All rights reserved.

Functional-Level Subtests

After the routing subtests are administered and scored, the examiner turns to the appropriate starting level determined from the raw score routing tables on pages 5 and 6 of the record form. The levels can be identified from the color-bars printed at the bottom of each page of Item Book 2 (nonverbal, the first levels to be administered in the standard order) and Item Book 3 (verbal). Also, the routing tables identify the starting pages in the record form where the examiner begins recording scores. Basal and ceiling rules are used to guide the assessment, and are printed at the top of each page of the record form. Each of the four subtests in the nonverbal domain will be discussed first, followed by the four subtests in the verbal domain. Recall that each subtest is composed of brief sets of items (the testlets) that are located in each of the four corners of the record form, with each corner representing a different cognitive ability.

After presenting each item, score the response using the answer key or directions included on the examiner direction pages of Item Book 2. Sum the item scores for each testlet and place the testlet raw score in the white box provided on the record form. The maximum score possible is nearly always 6 points (except for the two testlets at Nonverbal Level 1, which have 4 points each). Use the four raw-score totals on each page of the record form to implement the basal and ceiling rules printed at the top of each page where they are employed. No basal or ceiling rules are used at Nonverbal Level 1, which is the lowest level, or at the Nonverbal or Verbal Level 6, which concludes the test.

Nonverbal Functional-Level Subtests

The four nonverbal testlets are Knowledge, in the upper left corner of the record form; Quantitative Reasoning, in the lower left; Visual-Spatial Processing, in the upper right; and, finally, Working Memory, in the lower right. Administer the testlets in the order just stated—as if you were reading a two-column newspaper. Only Level 1 (for extremely low scores of 0 to 6 on Object Series/Matrices) has two testlets, for Visual-Spatial Processing and Working Memory, due to the lack of development of knowledge and quantitative concepts in the 2-year-old range. Subtests are, therefore, composed of a series of testlets located across levels (raw scores will be added together for the total subtest raw score). Most examiners test only about two levels (two complete pages of the record form), and possibly one or two additional testlets at a third level. Reversal to the previous level (when testlet raw scores are less than 3 points, or

DON'T FORGET

Basal and Ceiling Rules for the Functional-Levels Testlets

- *Basal rules* make sure that the examinee has started slightly below his or her ability level, allowing good measurement to be obtained.
- *Ceiling rules* determine when the examinee has reached his or her highest ability level on the test.
- Note that the rules for ceiling and basal shift slightly at Level 5.
- Use the total raw scores for each testlet (see the white raw-score boxes on the record form, pages 6 to 16, and fill in a sum of item scores ranging from 0 to 6).
- Note that Nonverbal Level 1 has maximum testlet scores of 4 whereas all other levels have maximum scores of 6.
- Basal and ceiling rules apply to each of the four cognitive factors (the four corners of the record form) separately so that testing is fair for examinees that have strengths in one or more of the cognitive factors.
- Basal rules apply *only* to the initial starting point determined from the routing table. Except for Level 5, the basal rule is to drop back one level for each factor testlet (each corner of the record form) where the raw score is low—2, 1, or 0 points.
- The basal rule at Level 5 is to drop back for low raw scores of 3, 2, 1, or 0.
- Ceiling rules also apply to each cognitive factor (each corner of the record form) separately. Stop testing a given factor when the testlet raw score is low (2 or fewer points) for *all* levels. Continue testing any factors with raw scores above 2 by continuing to the next page of the record form (only the corner or corners of the form where the ceiling has not yet been reached).
- Examiners have found that they usually test only 2 or 3 levels of nonverbal and 2 to 3 levels of verbal.

less than 4 points at Level 5) rarely occurs because the starting levels have been designed to occur below the examinee's actual level of ability.

Nonverbal Knowledge.   All the items in this subtest are scored correct (1) or incorrect (0). At the lowest level (Level 2), Procedural Knowledge testlets employ either the Child Card or a series of "Show me how you . . ." questions requiring the examinee to gesture to show understanding of the action requested. At Level 3, pictures in Item Book 2 are stimuli for questions of "Show me what you do with this." Again, the examinee gestures to show understanding of the action. Increasingly difficult Picture Absurdities appear in Levels 4, 5, and 6. Examinees "point and tell" what is silly or impossible about an aspect of the pictures, using brief verbalizations and gestures to communicate. Note that Picture Absurdities is the least nonverbal of this domain, but studies show that even second-language examinees are generally able to communicate the silliness of the pictures with the help of gestures.

Nonverbal Quantitative Reasoning.   All the items are straightforward to administer and are objectively scored using 0-1 scoring. Note that the first item in each testlet will have some degree of teaching, demonstration, or feedback (as with all SB5 subtests) to assure that each examinee understands the tasks being presented. Level 2 (the first level for this subtest) emphasizes manipulatives such as the counting rods (comparison of length) or blocks (placed in a cup) to assess emerging quantitative concepts. Have the plastic tray ready for accessing the pieces needed for each item. Level 3 features addition (using blocks) and number recognition. Items 3 and 4 of Level 3 require use of the Layout Card (turned with the black-and-white side, not the colored side, toward the examinee) to shield the movement of blocks. Levels 4, 5, and 6 use pictures to present increasingly complex mathematical concepts, sequences, and problems. The scoring, however, remains objective (the examinee must point to the answer on Item Book 2) and is easy for the examiner.

Nonverbal Visual-Spatial Processing.   This is the only nonverbal subtest that uses 0, 1, 2 multipoint scoring. The first two levels of the subtest

CAUTION

Examiner Tips for Administration of the Nonverbal Functional-Level Subtests

Nonverbal Knowledge

- On Item 1 in Level 2, the examinee may attempt to gesture "feeding" to self or examiner. Remind that the motion must be directed to the Child Card, but count the response as correct.

- Items are not timed in Procedural Knowledge, but research showed that young children rarely exceeded 20 s to respond; hence the use of a maximum time for the picture-gesture items.

- On Picture Absurdities, if the examinee explains the answer but does not point to the correct portion of the picture, say "Show me (again)" as a reminder that pointing is also required (otherwise, the correctness of the answer remains vague in some cases).

- A correct nonvocal response is possible through pointing and pantomime for the examinee with limited language. In the extreme case of inability to communicate in an older, higher functioning individual, the subtest may be spoiled, and prorating of the Nonverbal IQ is possible by using the conversions in the *Examiner's Manual* for only four nonverbal subtests.

Nonverbal Quantitative Reasoning

- Have the counting rods, blocks, and other manipulatives available in the plastic tray provided in the kit (with lid open and placed out of sight, such as on a side chair in easy reach).

- If the examinee does not point to answers but only responds vocally, prompt him or her to "Show me" by pointing to the answer on Item Book 2, as was required in the standardization of the SB5.

- On Item 1, Level 3, the examinee is allowed to pick up and compare the counting rods.

- Beginning at Level 4, Item 2, use the examiner prompt at 120 s, and then the second prompt at 180 s.

- Have pencil and scratch paper available for Levels 5 and 6.

(continued)

Nonverbal Visual-Spatial Processing

- For items using the Form Board, the board is sometimes rotated 90 or 180 deg. To prevent the examinee from moving the board you may have to gently place your hand on the board and signal "No."

- On Form Patterns (Levels 3 to 6), do not place the record form anywhere in the examinee's view because the correct designs are shown on the form.

- A quick scoring guide (see details in Rapid Reference 2.3) is that a perfect design gets 2 points, "close" with the Gestalt present but one to two errors present gets 1 point, and "not even close" with three or more errors gets 0 points.

- If the examinee says something like "I'm not good at designs," try to give some verbal encouragement about giving his or her best effort.

Nonverbal Working Memory

- Directions for Delayed Response (toys under the cups) are written from the examiner's viewpoint (e.g., "Place it under the cup to your right").

- When using the Layout Card at Level 1, use the black-and-white side toward the examinee and hold the card with both hands to screen out the examinee's view of the cups.

- On Block Span (Levels 2 to 6) use the extra block to tap, never your fingers (examinee does the same). Use an exaggerated "hopping" motion and the corner of the block to make each tap at 1-s intervals, to assure that the examinee sees each tap clearly.

- Placing the block in the examinee's hand, back and forth, is equivalent to the direction of placing the block on the table.

- Take time to mentally practice each tapping sequence (even if the examinee has to pause and wait) so that accuracy is obtained.

- Use your best creative, animated teaching on the sample items where taps are divided into the two rows. If you have effectively taught the separation of taps and used the examiner prompts printed in Item Book 2, and the examinee still does not catch the idea of the separate rows, he or she may be either distracted or not developmentally ready for the task.

Source: Reproduced from the *Stanford-Binet Fifth Edition, Examiner's Manual* by Gale H. Roid, Ph.D., with permission of the publisher. Copyright © 2003 by The Riverside Publishing Company. All rights reserved.

focus on the classic Form Board and correct placement of pieces, scored either completely correct (1 point) or incorrect (0 points). Quickly assemble the pieces into the Form Board to begin each item. Practice the assembly in advance and have the plastic tray and Form Board within reach as you prepare to test. On items requiring a rotation of the board, the examinee is not allowed to move the board. For Levels 3 through 6, Form Patterns provides a new style of visual puzzle unique to intelligence testing. The Form Board pieces were expanded to 10 pieces, including a parallelogram shape. Designs are shown on Item Book 2 without all pieces completely connected to each other and the examinee must assemble the design from the separate pieces. After experimentation with several ways of having examinees move the pieces, the SB5 development team found the most effective method to be the use of freeform, recognizable shapes (child, face, various animals, car, etc.) scored on a simple 2, 1, 0 rating. The designs can be assembled at any orientation by the examinee—they do not have to be perpendicular to the item-book picture, as when the examinee is left-handed and orients the design with the top to his or her right. The important thing for examiners to watch for is the emergence of the overall design—the Gestalt, or whole view of the design. Basically, 2 points are given when the whole is present and the design is nearly perfect with no missing or added pieces. Scores of 1 point are given for one to two errors (or disheveled or slightly separated or rotated pieces), and 0 points for three or more errors and lack of resemblance to the design. More details of scoring are given in expanded form in Rapid Reference 2.3.

Nonverbal Working Memory

At Level 1, the classic "shell game," called Delayed Response, is used. Toys are placed under plastic cups and the cups rotated with the task to identify which cup holds the toy—a measure of short-term memory. At Levels 2 and 3, the green blocks are used in a memory task in which the examinee taps the blocks in the same order as the examiner. Blocks

≡ Rapid Reference 2.3

Scoring of Form Patterns
(Nonverbal Visual-Spatial Processing, Levels 3 to 6)

General Scoring Directions

• You are looking for the whole figure or design (the Gestalt), such as an identifiable child or animal, to be clearly visible.

• Use the correct designs shown on the record form and the scoring examples shown on Item Book 2 in comparison to the examinee's design.

• In the development of the SB5, any designs that confused examinees or examiners and did not have good interexaminer reliability were dropped from the test, so the remaining designs should be easy to score.

• The overall orientation of the design (e.g., tipped to the right for a left-handed examinee or tipped to the left for a right-hander) does *not* affect scoring as long as the whole design is intact.

2-Point Responses

• Either a perfect or near-perfect design with all pieces present and only slight rotation of freestanding pieces will receive full 2-point credit. *Freestanding* means that the piece does not touch another piece along a complete edge, but only at a corner, small area, or not at all. For example, on Item 1 of Level 3 (walking person composed of four pieces), all the pieces are freestanding.

• When the whole (Gestalt, recognizable design) and all correct pieces are present, slight rotations of freestanding pieces does not affect scoring. For example, on Item 3 of Level 3 (face), slight rotations of less than 10 deg on the eyebrows would not disqualify a 2-point score.

1-Point Responses

• Give 1 point for designs that are slightly messy (disheveled) and/or contain 1–2 missing or misplaced pieces.

• When the whole design (the Gestalt) is recognizable but messy, slight rotations, shifted, or disheveled pieces are allowed for a

1-point response when the rotations do not exceed more than 45 deg. For example, on Item 3 at Level 3 (face), the mouth could be curved in a slight smile (and thus be disheveled) but still allowed. If one of the eyebrow triangles were switched with the nose triangle, and the mouth was a smile, there would be two misplaced pieces and disheveled appearance of the mouth—still earning a 1-point score.

- See the examples of 1-point responses in Item Book 2.

0-Point Responses

- Use a zero score when three or more pieces are missing, switched, or misplaced.
- Use a zero score when you cannot identify the design—the Gestalt is missing (e.g., it looks like only half a face on Item 3, Level 3, or the kite is missing on Item 2, Level 3).
- Use a zero score if the examinee exceeds the time limit without completing the design sufficiently (three or more pieces missing, switched, or misplaced).

Special Notes

- Using two half-circles to make a circle, or two rectangles to make a square, is allowed if the overall design (Gestalt) is clearly present, and the pieces are not needed elsewhere in the design.
- Alternative correct solutions are possible on the goose, boat, and car found in Levels 5 and 6.

Scoring Tips

- The summary of the scoring criteria is as follows: Use 2 points for a perfect or near-perfect design, 1 point when two or fewer errors exist, and 0 points when the design is not even close to the person, animal, or object intended.
- Based on examinee performance on previous levels and other testlets, you will probably begin to see the examinee shift from 2-point to 1-point to 0-point responses as he or she reaches a personal ceiling, at which the designs become too difficult.
- Practice the designs yourself so that you are familiar with the teaching examples (the first designs on Levels 3, 4, and 5) and also to understand the challenges and pitfalls of assembling the correct design.

should be tapped in a smooth, 1-second-per-tap sequence. The blocks are placed on the colored side of the Layout Card where numbers are printed (to be facing the examiner only) to guide the examiner's tapping sequence. Examiners should practice the tapping sequences before giving official assessments. Also, it is wise to take a few seconds to practice the tap sequences mentally by scanning the record form where the numbers for each sequence are printed. Neither the examiner nor the examinee needs to vocalize the numbers—they are only for the use of the examiner. Thus, the task is similar to the digit-span task, because the idea is to test the memory span of the examinee, but conducted in the visual-spatial mode instead of verbal-numerical. Sample teaching items are used to assure that the examinee understands the task. Beginning at the middle of Level 3, an innovative working-memory version of Block Span is employed. In this task, the examinee is taught to separate the taps in the lighter yellow row first, and then the taps in the darker red row. An example of the sequence 5-1-6-2 is shown in Rapid Reference 2.4. The examiner first shows the full sequence, 5-1-6-2, then teaches the separation of the first-row taps, 1-2 (in the lighter yellow row, nearest the examinee), and then the taps in the second row, 5-6 (in the darker red row, farthest from examinee). All taps in both rows must be correct

≡Rapid Reference 2.4

Example of Block Span Administration Procedures at the Higher Levels

Examinee is on this side

Yellow row (four blocks)	1[b]	2[d]	3	4
Red row (four blocks)	5[a]	6[c]	7	8

Examiner is located here

Note: Lowercase letters show the sequence of block taps by the examiner (a-b-c-d). The correct sequence of taps by the examinee would be b-d-a-c (1-2-5-6).

to obtain the item score of 1 point. The examiner need only be watchful for a single mistake to determine the appropriate score. However, some examiners may find rich clinical information by observing complete response patterns even when incorrect. The number of taps is progressively increased through successive test levels.

CAUTION

Examiner Tips for Administration of the Verbal Functional-Level Subtests

Verbal Knowledge

- Organize the toys and Child Card in advance when testing lower levels.
- The examinee's proper articulation or pronunciation is not important—only whether the definition and content are correct.
- Two of the words (Items 34 and 37) have two acceptable pronunciations.
- Be sure to note the base points in calculating the raw score because they are more complex with the 0, 1, and 2 option scoring.

Verbal Quantitative Reasoning

- At the lowest level (Level 2) examinees can signal or use fingers or blocks, but they *must* additionally speak or count orally to receive full credit.
- Try not to show favoritism for math problems that you feel the child will like more (e.g., those with pictures).
- Have the counting rods, blocks, and so on handy in the plastic tray.
- Higher level items (Levels 4 to 6) will have the examiner prompt to move the examinee forward when stalled.

Verbal Visual-Spatial Processing

- Block placement is counted correct when at least half of the block surface is placed correctly on the target object (for Level 2, any place on the bottom half of the house on Item 4 is correct).

(continued)

- Use a query ("Tell me about your answer") if the examinee places the block in an odd location in Level 3.
- You can leave a block on the item book page and have the examinee move it around from item to item.
- For higher levels (Levels 5 and 6) you can repeat the wording of the Position and Direction items one time (since this is not a memory task).
- To score the higher level items (Levels 5 and 6) involving turns (right, left, north, south), define a right turn from north to east, for example, as a 90-deg turn. A turn from north to northeast would be a 45-deg turn.
- Taking shortcuts (such as cutting across the grass) when giving directions at Level 5) is never correct. Say, "No, stick to the path."

Verbal Working Memory

- You do not need to copy the examinee's response exactly on Memory for Sentences (or the complete answers to questions on Last Word) unless there is something unusual about the wording that might suggest future interventions or speech or language difficulties.
- If you suspect a hearing difficulty in the examinee, be sure to call for a separate hearing assessment, ask the caregivers, or check records. This subtest may require accommodations for individuals with deafness.
- Elderly individuals may request repetition of items, but explain that "We are looking at memory for the first time you hear it."
- The examinee may spontaneously rehearse answers during the giving of the complete item (and this may actually distract them!).
- Provide time for the examinee's response, but do not have lengthy pauses between the memory items.

Verbal Functional-Level Subtests

Beginning on page 12 of the record form, use Item Book 3 to administer the verbal levels portion of the SB5, based on the raw score obtained from the Vocabulary subtest. As in the nonverbal levels, each page has four testlets. The standard administration sequence follows the method of reading a two-column newspaper—Fluid Reasoning in the upper left corner first, then Quantitative Reasoning in the lower left, then Visual-Spatial Processing in the upper right, and Working Memory in the lower right. Unlike in the nonverbal section, Fluid Reasoning now occurs in the upper left because Verbal Knowledge was previously measured by the Vocabulary routing subtest and verbal reasoning was not measured by the Object Series/Matrices routing subtest. Note that there is no Level 1 for the verbal section, because verbal abilities are not well developed in the typical 2-year-old or low-functioning individual.

Verbal Fluid Reasoning

This subtest uses multipoint scoring (usually 0, 1, and 2). Level 2 uses a series of pictures on Item Book 3 to stimulate the examinee to describe the interaction going on in the pictured scene. The examiner should be looking for the examinee's understanding that there is cause and effect, or interaction between characters, going on in the pictures—not simply identification of objects, which does not qualify as reasoning per se. Use of pictures such as these goes back to early editions of the Stanford-Binet.

At Level 3, a very unique sorting game is used, and it is the one verbal subtest that takes more time to learn and administer. The task for the examinee is to sort the blue and yellow chips based on the details or meanings of the pictures on the chips. Begin by placing all 30 chips on the table with pictures turned upward. Teach the concept of "groups of three that go together" by separating three red pictures—the red rose, red apple, and red bird. Practice in advance and separate these pieces in the plastic tray so that they are readily available when testing begins. After demonstration of these three chips, place them back into the set of 30 (mix them randomly on the table), and say, "I want you to find three other chips that go together and tell me how they are all alike." Further instructions are included in Item Book 3, page 15, where several feedback prompts are used to assure that the rules of the sorting game are

CAUTION

Nonverbal Levels 3 to 6, Working Memory (Block Span)

Examiners should follow some important tips for proper administration of the advanced tapping sequences:

- Most of the SB5 subtests are easy to learn and administer. The advanced Block Span items require some additional guidelines.
- Be sure you have eye contact with the examinee as you teach her or him the game of tapping blocks in the yellow row first, then the blocks in the red row. Use animated gesturing and enthusiasm to teach the separation of yellow and red rows, following the wording for examiner prompts in the Item Book 2. If the examinee does not properly separate the two rows of taps after repeated reminders, perhaps he or she is not advanced in working-memory processes. The examinee may have difficulty with attention or following directions.
- Read the directions carefully, and practice well before official testing begins.
- Tap with the corner of the tapping block to get a crisp sound and accurate tap.
- Tap slowly using a 1-s interval. Use an exaggerated hopping motion to be sure the examinee follows each tap.
- Take a few seconds to mentally rehearse the tap sequence before giving each item, even if the examinee has to wait. Use the tapping numbers printed in the record form, gazing back and forth from the record form to the layout card and blocks.

clear to the examinee. Note that the scoring of this testlet results in raw scores from 0 to 6, but in a unique way, using the conversion table on page 13 of the record form. Obviously, unlike the simple multiple-choice tasks in most of the other SB5 testlets, this Early Reasoning task will take some practice in advance of official use. Practice for yourself by trying all possible groupings of three chips to become familiar with the task. Most examiners find this task highly diagnostic, as did neuropsychological researchers who developed similar "category" tasks.

Level 4 assesses Fluid Reasoning with a classic Stanford-Binet task, Verbal Absurdities. Examinees listen to verbal statements from the examiner that are absurd in some manner. The examinee is directed to explain why the statement is silly or impossible. This task begins with a learning item to ensure that the examinee understands the task. Responses are written in the record form and scored according to the 2, 1, 0 guidelines. The item book presents the examiner with multiple examples of responses warranting the different scores. Examinees may be prompted to provide more clarity to their responses when score determinations are questionable. The examiner may say "Tell me more" to prompt this clarification. Levels 5 and 6 use the classic Verbal Analogies task to assess verbal reasoning. Now examinees are presented with a verbal and visual prompt of a sentence such as "_____ is to SIZE as ROSE is to _____" (Correct answer: "*Small* is to SIZE as ROSE is to *flower*.") These verbal analogies are contrasted by the nonverbal analogies occurring within the Object Series/Matrices subtest. Verbal Analogies is scored with a 2, 1, 0 scale. For a 2-point score, the examinee's response should correctly complete both sides of the analogy statement in proper sequence. A 1-point response occurs with analogy sentences that are partially correct, that mix elements of two different analogies when only one is possible, or that reverse the proper sequence. Incorrect 0-point responses provide some association with the provided terms without an apparent connection of associations. The scoring

CAUTION

Verbal Level 3 has slightly different scoring rules for Fluid Reasoning.

Note that Fluid Reasoning at Verbal Level 3 (sorting chips) is slightly different in scoring. There are 10 possible ways to sort the chips into groups of three each, but the number of sorts is transformed into a final raw score ranging from 1 to 6 (see the point table on page 13 of the record form). Also, note that the examiner directions printed on Item Book 3 include a number of feedback messages to help the examinee understand the rules of the sorting game.

rules and examples of responses are provided on the examiner direction pages of Item Book 3 and in an expanded appendix in the *Examiner's Manual.*

Verbal Quantitative Reasoning

Quantitative Reasoning items are scored as either correct (1 point) or incorrect (0 points) through levels 2 through 6. Each level begins with a teaching item. Quantitative Reasoning begins in the verbal domain at Level 2 with a testlet where examinees count toys and other objects. The red counting rods and green blocks are utilized in addition to other intriguing small-toy objects. Instructions provided within the item book are simple and give examples of appropriate corrective feedback at the first item. This testlet begins with a very basic assessment of the examinee's ability to count.

In Level 3, Quantitative Reasoning incorporates number naming and basic addition and subtraction tasks. Items incorporate pictorial objects and brief word problems. It is important to follow the item book prompts rather than rephrasing these items, to maintain their psychometric properties. Assessment in these areas should maintain a standardized administration style, rather than slipping into colloquial speech to introduce items.

Level 4 increases Quantitative Reasoning difficulty by including concepts of measurement as well as geometric and word problems. Examinees will need to utilize logic and multiplication skills to produce a verbal response. Some items incorporate the counting rods and green blocks. Examinees do not have the option of utilizing paper and pencil to work out mathematical solutions. Then, in Level 5, Quantitative Reasoning examinees are provided with paper and pencil as problems become increasingly complex. Word problems become complex and incorporate high-level mathematical reasoning. Administration demands in Levels 5 and 6 are relatively simple. There are no manipulatives to present and the simple item directions have little variability. In Level 6 the mathematical complexity and reasoning demanded with each item is increased. Remember that these items are scored either correct or incorrect: 1 or 0.

Verbal Visual-Spatial Processing

Although the subtest name *Position and Direction* may be new to the SB5, several of the tasks have appeared on previous editions of Stanford-Binet. At the lowest levels (Levels 2 and 3), the examinee moves objects (ball or block) onto Item Book 3 (laid flat on the table) in response to verbal commands to place the object "on," "inside," "in front of," and so on. The use of the objects seems to help children and lower-functioning individuals engage in the game-like nature of the tasks. You will often hand the examinee a block and ask her or him to place it on the item book in response to the question. Higher level items (Levels 5 and 6) are derived from classic Stanford-Binet items called "Orientation: Direction." They require the examinee to listen to a series of directional turns (*left, right,* and *north, south*) and visualize the final orientation when all turns are completed.

Verbal Working Memory

This subtest begins with the classic Memory for Sentences, which has been with the Binet tests since the beginning. The examinee repeats word-for-word the sentences read to him or her by the examiner. Simple sentences with few words progress to longer sentences. Perfect reproduction of the sentence gets the examinee 2 points. A sentence repeated with only one word wrong gets 1 point and two or more words incorrect gets 0 points. At Level 4, the task shifts to the Last Word activity adapted from the research by Daneman and Carpenter (1980). Brief questions are read to the examinee (like the question, "Is the earth square?"), requiring a "yes" or "no" response, but the answer is not scored. The questions serve only as interference to the main task of remembering the last word in each question (e.g., "square"). Teaching items introduce the task and train the examinee in the proper playing of the game and remembering the last words. As the levels increase, the number and length of sentences in each item progressively increases. The working memory aspect of the task is the mental sorting of the last words from all the other words in the series of questions held in short-term memory. Also, the examinee must avoid of the interference of the responses to each question. The task is extremely sensitive to brain dysfunction, attention problems, and serial memory disruptions.

SUMMARY OF TEST-ADMINISTRATION DESIGN FEATURES

As explained in this chapter, the SB5 tailors the assessment to the ability level of the examinee by doing an initial assessment (the two subtests in Item Book 1) and then using that information to begin testing at the appropriate levels in the nonverbal section (Item Book 2) and the verbal section (Item Book 3). The initial assessment, using Object Series/Matrices and Vocabulary, is reliable enough by itself that it produces an estimated ability score called the *Abbreviated Battery IQ*. The overall reliability of the full-scale assessment is greatly enhanced by this accurate, initial assessment, which allows the remainder of the test to be adapted to the examinee's functional level. Thus, examinee frustration is prevented by finding his or her appropriate level such that items are easy at first and then appropriately challenging as testing proceeds. Great care was taken in the development of the SB5 to study the effect on the examinee of the mixture of tasks at each level (in Item Books 2 and 3), with the conclusion that the mixture promoted greater interest and attention of the examinee during the testing process than the traditional point-scale format of other tests. By including the mixture of tasks at each level, the SB5 restored the original age-level design of the early Terman and Merrill (1937, 1960) editions, while bringing new psychometric technology to the design process. At the same time, the use of the easel design in the item books, with examiner directions printed on each page, made the levels design much easier for examiners to learn and apply as compared to earlier editions. Students and clinicians learning the SB5 can simply begin with Item Book 1 and page 3 of the record form and follow the directions on each page.

 TEST YOURSELF

1. **What is the standard order of SB5 test administration?**
   (a) Object Series/Matrices, nonverbal levels, Vocabulary, verbal levels
   (b) Nonverbal subtests, verbal subtests
   (c) Two routing subtests, nonverbal levels, verbal levels
   (d) Vocabulary, Object Series/Matrices, verbal levels, nonverbal levels

2. **Which of the SB5 subtests include multipoint item scoring (2, 1, or 0)?**
   (a) Nonverbal Fluid Reasoning
   (b) Nonverbal Knowledge
   (c) Nonverbal Quantitative Reasoning
   (d) Nonverbal Visual-Spatial Processing
   (e) Nonverbal Working Memory
   (f) Verbal Fluid Reasoning
   (g) Verbal Knowledge
   (h) Verbal Quantitative Reasoning
   (i) Verbal Visual-Spatial Processing
   (j) Verbal Working Memory

3. **Which of the rules is consistent across the functional levels of the SB5 (where the rule applies)?**
   (a) The basal rule
   (b) The ceiling rule

(continued)

4. **What is the most frequent *maximum* raw score possible for each of the testlets in the functional-level portions of the SB5?**

   (a) 4

   (b) 5

   (c) 6

   (d) 8

5. **Which reverse rule is true for the routing subtests?**

   (a) Go back to the previous item in the sequence.

   (b) Go back to the next lowest start point.

   (c) Go back to the previous item only when the initial score is less than 3.

6. **What is the primary benefit of establishing examinee rapport?**

   (a) Encouraging examinees to complete each testlet

   (b) Obtaining the most accurate testing performance

   (c) Keeping the examinee happy to ensure future testing referrals

7. **Which two subtests are utilized as routing subtests?**

   (a) Nonverbal Fluid Reasoning and Verbal Visual-Spatial Processing

   (b) Nonverbal Working Memory and Verbal Knowledge

   (c) Nonverbal Fluid Reasoning and Verbal Knowledge

   (d) Nonverbal Knowledge and Verbal Fluid Reasoning

8. **Rapport is somewhat beneficial, but not critical, in administering intelligence assessments.** True or False?

9. **Who is most likely to benefit from the game-like presentation of the testlets?**

   (a) The examiner

   (b) Young children and very low functioning adults

   (c) Highly intelligent young adults

10. **Which SB5 subtest includes a testlet in which picture chips are sorted into categories?**

Answers: 1. c; 2. d, f, g, j; 3. b; 4. c; 5. b; 6. b; 7. c; 8. False; 9. b; 10. Verbal Fluid Reasoning

Three

HOW TO SCORE THE SB5

HAND SCORING FOR NORMATIVE COMPARISONS

The standard method of hand scoring for the SB5 is very similar to that of other cognitive batteries. Raw scores for each section of the test are summed across the scores for each item and converted into normative standard scores using appendix tables in the *Examiner's Manual* (Roid, 2003c). As discussed in Chapter 2, item scores are usually coded 0 for incorrect and 1 for correct so the raw score totals are easy to obtain in the interior of the SB5 record form. Raw scores are first totaled for each subtest—straightforwardly in the routing subtests of Item Book 1 and involving the accumulation of testlet scores within the levels sections of Item Books 2 and 3, as described in Chapter 2.

Raw scores are difficult to interpret until they have been transformed to normative scores or other supplemental derived scores. Normative scores include scaled scores ranging from 1 to 19 for subtests and standard scores ranging from approximately 40 to 160 (average 100) for factors and IQ composites. Each of the steps in normative scoring will be described in this chapter. Supplemental methods of scoring the SB5 include computer scoring; optional transformation of raw scores into Change-Sensitive Scores leading to age equivalent scores; and various conversions of normative scores to percentiles. Each of these scoring methods will be described in this chapter.

Checking the Accuracy of Raw Scores

Before proceeding to normative scoring, it is always wise to double-check the accuracy of the raw scores you have calculated within the record form. Check the raw scores for Object Series/Matrices (the Nonverbal Fluid Reasoning subtest) and Vocabulary (the Verbal Knowledge subtest) first. Be sure that you have given credit for nonadministered items prior to the starting point (the base points) and add them to the earned points from actual

> # CAUTION
>
> ....
>
> Examiners should be aware that clerical errors on test record forms are among the most frequent errors in assessment. Know the scoring criteria in advance of administering the SB5 and check all calculations for reasonableness. This can be particularly important when testing examinees for important life decisions such as qualification for special education, Workers Compensation, or Social Security. Check item scoring, basal or ceiling rules, and transcription of scores from page to page.

items administered. Be sure that you properly employed the stopping rule—four consecutive incorrect responses (0 scores)—in both routing subtests. For the functional-level testlets, check to see that none of them exceeds 6 points (4 points for Nonverbal Level 1), especially Verbal Level 3, Fluid Reasoning (sorting chips), which has a special conversion table.

Normative Scaled Scores for Subtests

The most widely used scores on intelligence batteries are the standard scores derived from a comparison of raw scores to the performance of age groups from the nationally representative norm sample of the test. For subtests, these normative scores are centered at 10 for the mean raw score obtained nationally by a given age group. The spread (standard

DON'T FORGET

- ...to add the base points to the actual earned points in the routing subtests.
- ...to mark and add the points for testlets at a lower level than the starting level for the nonverbal and verbal levels section of the test (see the shaded numbers printed on the scoring boxes of the front page of the record form).
- ...that Object Series/Matrices has a total maximum score of 36 points from 36 one-point items.
- ...that Vocabulary has 14 one-point items at the lower level and 30 one- or two-point items at the upper level, for a total maximum score of 74.
- ...to copy the total scores of the routing subtests to the proper columns of the scoring boxes on the record form (those with bold arrows shown in color and marked with the word "Routing").
- ...to accurately transcribe all testlet scores to the proper scoring box on the front page of the record form.
- ...after completing the transcribing of testlet scores, to verify that the ceiling rule was properly applied to all subtests.

deviation) of scores is converted to a standard 3 points. This allows all of the subtests (regardless of the number of raw score points) to be compared with one another in the subtest profile. Scores range from a low of 1 to a high of 19, with the average at 10. Because these scores are created to fit a normal curve, most of examinees will fall within the middle range of 7 to 13 points (one standard deviation in each direction of the mean).

Also, very few examinees obtain scores of either 1 or 19, at the extremes of the normal distribution. Even though there may be several raw scores possible at the extreme points (scaled scores of 1 and 19), all raw scores that would be converted to a number below 1 are converted to scaled scores of 1, and all raw scores above 19 are converted to 19.

DON'T FORGET

Be careful to complete the summary tables of the nonverbal and verbal functional-level subtests on the first page of the SB5 record form (upper left corner). Enter the tables at the level of the examinee's starting point for the nonverbal domain and, separately, for the verbal domain. Note that the starting-point levels may be different between the two domains. The numbers 4 and 6 that appear in shaded printing are the maximum values that can be entered. Be sure to credit the examinee for the levels below his or her starting point.

Examiners should keep these limits in mind when interpreting scores of extremely low functioning or high functioning individuals, and consider using supplemental scoring for those examinees.

To complete the profile of subtest scaled scores on the front page of the record form, follow the example in Figure 3.1. First, enter the raw scores for each of the routing subtests—where the large downward arrows are printed on the raw score tables. The abbreviation FR in the nonverbal table stands for Fluid Reasoning, which is the Object Series/Matrices subtest; KN in the verbal table stands for Knowledge, which is the Vocabulary subtest. Take the raw score totals for these subtests (from pages 3 and 5 of the record form) and write them below the tips of their respective arrows.

For the functional-level testlets (which add together to form the nonrouting subtests), notice the lightly printed numbers on the record form in the area shown by Figure 3.1. As mentioned previously, the maximum score for testlets is usually 6, except for the Nonverbal Level 1 testlets, which have a maximum of 4. These maximum scores will be credited to your examinee for any testlets below the starting level of your assessment in Item Books 2 and 3. First, identify the testlet raw scores from the level you started in Item Book 2 (nonverbal). For example, if you started at Level 2 and the examinee received raw scores of 5, 5, 3, and 5, you would enter these in the line marked Level 2 using the four boxes to the right of the arrow symbol for routing (the KN, QR

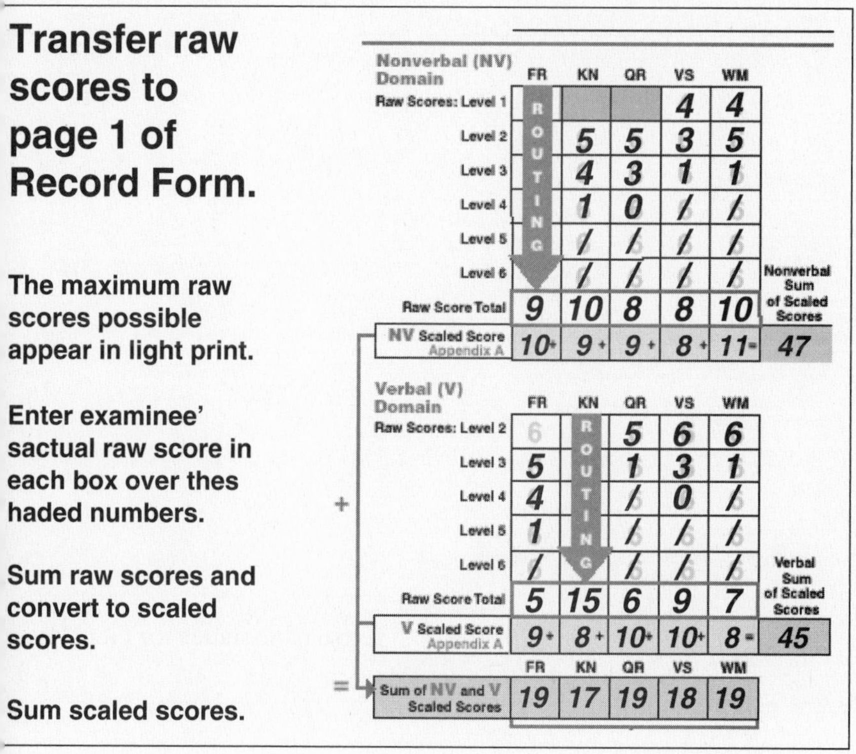

Transfer raw scores to page 1 of Record Form.

The maximum raw scores possible appear in light print.

Enter examinee'sactual raw score in each box over thes haded numbers.

Sum raw scores and convert to scaled scores.

Sum scaled scores.

Figure 3.1 Example of hand scoring for the subtest scores (both routing and levels subtests)

Source: Reproduced from the SB5 University Training Resources, Power Point Presentation with permission of the publisher. Copyright © 2003 by The Riverside Publishing Company. All rights reserved.

[Quantitative Reasoning], VS [Visual-Spatial Processing], and WM [Working Memory] testlets, in that order). Next you would fill in the maximum scores of 4 for VS and WM at Level 1 because you give credit to the examinee for these lower-level, easy testlets. Then, you would complete Level 3 and Level 4 if those were reached by the examinee. In most cases, examinees are administered only two or three levels of testlets before they reach a ceiling, so you would probably not have testlet scores for Levels 5 and 6 in this case. Any levels not reached can be left blank or marked with a slash. The final step in calculating the functional-level subtests is to sum each column downward, placing the total raw score across levels (including the base points from low levels before the starting level) and placing the total in the row labeled "Raw Score Total."

Scaled scores are obtained for each subtest raw score total by using the norm tables in the appendix of the *Examiner's Manual*. Find the appropriate age range for your examinee, then identify the raw scores within the body of the table, and trace your finger to the right or left to retrieve the scaled score printed on the side columns. Write the scaled scores for each subtest in the appropriate box on the record form (near the bottom of the nonverbal and verbal sections of Fig. 3.1).

Composite Standard Scores

Composite scores are calculated from the sums of various combinations of subtest scaled scores. They include the scores for each of the five cognitive factors (Fluid Reasoning, Knowledge, Quantitative Reasoning, Visual-Spatial Processing, Working Memory) and are called *Factor Index scores*, each derived from the sum of two subtest scaled scores (the nonverbal and verbal subtests for each factor). Two composite scores are derived from the sum of the five nonverbal subtest scaled scores (*Nonverbal IQ*, or *NVIQ*) or the five verbal subtest scaled scores (*Verbal IQ*, or *VIQ*). The most complete composite score, the *Full Scale IQ* (*FSIQ*), is derived from the sum of all 10 subtest scaled scores. Follow the directional arrows printed on the Record Form, summing downward for factors and across the bottom row (marked "NV Scaled Score" or "V Scaled Score" in Fig. 3.1) to obtain the sums of scaled scores for the composites. Go to the appendix tables for the composite scores in the *Examiner's Manual* to obtain the conversion of sums to Factor Index or IQ scores.

Supplemental Scoring

Three supplemental scoring options are offered with the SB5: the Abbreviated Battery IQ (ABIQ), the Change-Sensitive Scores (CSSs), and the Extended IQ (EXIQ). The ABIQ and the EXIQ are normative scores comparing the examinee's performance to the norm sample. The CSSs, available for the SB5 composites, provide a unique scoring system that is useful for tracking improvement or decline in cognitive functions over time and other advantages (discussed shortly).

Abbreviated IQ

The two routing subtests in Item Book 1—Object Series/Matrices and Vocabulary—can be combined to form an estimated IQ, called the *Abbreviated Battery IQ* (*ABIQ*). The ABIQ is a standard score converted from the sum of the scaled scores for the two routing subtests. A section on page 2 of the SB5 record form provides directions for calculating the estimated IQ. The ABIQ is formed from subtests that estimate two important cognitive factors—Fluid Reasoning (Object Series/Matrices) and Knowledge or crystallized ability (Vocabulary)—according to the widely recognized theory of Cattell (1943) and Horn (1994). Assessment professionals should be cautious in using the ABIQ, given that it is less reliable than the FSIQ and covers only two of the five cognitive factors measured by the SB5. However, when available assessment time is short and other cognitive batteries are being given as part of a comprehensive assessment of an individual, the ABIQ has a role in providing a global estimate of intellectual level.

Change-Sensitive Scores

Another conversion of raw scores, the CSS, provides a different type of scale interpretable in terms of age equivalents and task difficulty. Thus, the CSSs are referenced to the criteria of developmental level (age) and the complexity of tasks; hence they are "criterion-referenced" (Berk,

1984; Cohen & Swerdlik, 1999) scales. As shown in Figure 3.2, CSSs are calculated from the raw score sums rather than the sums of scaled scores. An alternative set of tables in an alternative appendix of the *Examiner's Manual* is used to convert the scores. As seen in the bottom three lines of Figure 3.2, the CSSs fall in the 400 to 500 range, with each score having an estimated error (SE, or standard error) as well as an age equivalent. The scores typically range from about 430 for a 2-year-old to about 520 for an adult. The scores have been centered at 500 for age 10 years zero months, as developed by Richard Woodcock (1999). Similar to the scale of the Scholastic Aptitude Test (SAT; College Entrance Ex-

Change-Sensitive Scores (CSSs)

- **Optional scoring method**
- **Useful when evaluating extreme performance levels (high or low) or documenting growth**
- **Consult Roid (2003c) to obtain the CSS, standard error, and age equivalent for composites**

Calculation of Change-Sensitive Scores and Age Equivalents

To calculate the change-sensitive scores (CSS), first record the raw scores from the previous page for the appropriate subtests. Then sum the column scores for each factor and the row scores for each IQ. Locate the appropriate tables in Appendix C to determine each change-sensitive score, *SE*, and corresponding age equivalent.

	FR	KM	QR	VS	WM	NV	V	FS
NV Raw Score Total	9 +	10 +	8 +	8 +	10	=45		
V Raw Score Total	5 +	15 +	6 +	9 +	7	=		
Factor Raw Score Total	14 +	25 +	14 +	17 +	17	=		87
Appendix C CSS	457	453	433	450	447	451		457
SE	49	5	5	5	5	3		2
Age Equivalent	4-1	3-8	3-8	3-11	4-0	3-10		3-9

Change-Sensitive Scores (CSS) for the Abbreviated Battery (AB)

	AB
NV FR Raw Score Total	9
V KN Raw Score Total	15
Sum of Raw Scores	24
Appendix C CSS	459
SE	4
Age Equivalent	3-9

Figure 3.2 Section of SB5 Record Form showing calculation of Change-Sensitive Scores

Source: Reproduced from the SB5 University Training Resources, Power Point Presentation with permission of the publisher. Copyright © 2003 by The Riverside Publishing Company. All rights reserved.

amination Board, 2003) used for college admissions, the meaning of the CSS values will gain importance and clarity over time. Users of the SAT know that 500 is the national average and that a combined score of more than 1,000 (verbal 500 plus quantitative 500) is often needed for admittance to an advanced college. In the same way, CSSs will gain meaning as more and more users apply the scores in assessments with the SB5 and other tests (e.g., Woodcock et al., 2001a, 2001b; Roid & Miller, 1997) employing the same metric. Rapid Reference 3.1 shows an example of CSS scaling for the Working Memory domain as derived by Pomplun (2003). Pomplun showed that increasing CSSs for Working Memory on the SB5 was directly related to the complexity of the sentences memorized in Verbal Working Memory, beginning with the Memory for Sentences and transitioning to the more difficult Last Word task. As CSSs increase for the older age groups (see age equivalence in Rapid Reference 3.1), the memory task gets more and more complex, from sentence lengths of 2 to 11 words in Memory for Sentences to combinations of 2 to 6 sentences in Last Word. Clearly, the higher the CSS, the more memory span and capability the examinee displays—a perfect example of a criterion-referenced scale (Berk, 1984). At the center point of 500 on the CSS scale, someone who is 9 years 11 months old is typically able to remember the last word from a series of three sentences.

CSS scales are useful in various important ways. First, the scores can be used to give feedback to parents or guardians of low-functioning individuals who always test at the very lowest percentile or IQ and who do not appear to improve from special instruction. The appearance of no change may be an artifact of the constantly shifting comparison of the individual to his or her age peers (who become more and more advanced as they get older). In actuality, at the item-score level, these low-functioning individuals may be gaining small increments of skill here and there. The CSS, being based on raw scores and having a broader range than most normative scores, may show change across time for these individuals. Second, individuals with traumatic brain injury or

Rapid Reference 3.1

Meaning of Change-Sensitive Scores (CSSs) for Verbal Working Memory

Age Equivalent	CSS	Verbal Test	Task
<2-0			
2-1	414	MFS 2-1	2 words
2-4			
2-5	421	MFS 2-2	3 words
3-1	432	MFS 2-3	4 words
3-4	436	MFS 4-1	5 words
4-1			
4-3	449	MFS 4-2	7 words
4-5			
4-8			
4-9			
4-11			
5-4	465	MFS 4-4	11 words
5-5			
5-6			
5-10			
6-7	479	LW 6-3	2 sentences
6-8	480	LW 6-4	2 sentences
7-2	485	LW 6-5	2 sentences
7-8			
7-10			
8-2			
9-1			

9-11	500	LW 8-2	3 sentences
11-6			
11-10			
12-5	511	LW 8-3	4 sentences
16-3			
16-3			
> 21-0	527	LW 8-4	5 sentences
> 21-0			
> 21-0	541	LW 10-2	5 sentences
> 21-0			
> 21-0	544	LW 10-4	6 sentences
> 21-0			
> 21-0	548	LW 10-3	6 sentences
> 21-0			

Notes: MFS = Memory for Sentences; LW = Last Word. Age equivalents are given in years and months.

Source: Pomplun (2003). Used by permission of the author and Riverside Publishing.

other neurological illnesses may show low performance on standard scores, but, with repeated testing across a period of years, show gains on the CSS. Finally, as shown in Rapid Reference 3.1, the CSS scales could be used to suggest possible instructional interventions, such as training examinees to master the next most difficult tasks at points above their current level on the CSS. For example, if an individual did have a CSS of 500 on Working Memory, sets of three, four, or even five sentences could be used in memory training (but *not* the SB5 sentences, of course, because it is unethical to "teach to the test") to stretch the boundaries of the individual's level of performance.

Extended IQ

Once the CSS values have been calculated, the Full Scale values (those derived from the sum of all 10 subtests) can be converted to a new ex-

> ## CAUTION
>
> Be cautious when tabulating scores. The SB5 Scoring Pro provides the most efficient and accurate method of obtaining all possible scores. The chance for examiner error increases every time a score is transferred from one page to another or when data are transferred from the tables. When establishing scores by hand it would be prudent to double-check to avoid error.

tension of the IQ scale. Conventional normative IQ scores are limited to the range of approximately 40 to 160 because of the nature of normalized standard scores. However, extreme cases exist with cognitive abilities (and raw scores) that can be projected beyond these boundaries. For these reasons, an innovative new *Extended IQ (EXIQ)* was developed for the SB5 and the conversion tables published in the *Interpretive Manual* (Roid, 2003d). When conventional IQ values are lower than 50 or greater than 150, the EXIQ provides an alternative estimate of IQ based on the sum of the raw scores rather than the sum of the scaled scores of the subtests. The EXIQ tables provide estimates from an extremely low 10 IQ to 39 IQ, and from 161 to an extreme of 225 IQ on the high end. Clearly, such scores should be used only in extreme cases, where, for example, a low-functioning person with mental retardation needs to be placed in 24-h care if his of her level of performance is exceedingly low.

COMPUTER SCORING

In addition to hand scoring, an optional computer-scoring program is available for the SB5: the SB5 Scoring Pro (Roid, 2003f). The program is distributed on compact disk (CD, IBM-compatible format) for use on a given computer for unlimited numbers of cases. By entering raw scores into the program, all of the normative and supplemental scores described previously can be derived for a given examinee. Also, a de-

≡ Rapid Reference 3.2

Features of the SB5 Computerized Scoring Program

- User-friendly screens and directions
- Various modes of data input and optional reporting formats
- Instant retrieval of normative scores and calculation of composites and score differences
- Optional input of Woodcock-Johnson III Tests of Achievement scores and calculation of ability-achievement discrepancy analysis
- Ability to export brief narrative reports and graphs to a word processor for further editing or combining with other reports

Source: The SB5 Scoring Pro manual, published by Riverside Publishing, 425 Spring Lake Drive, Itasca, IL 60143 (Roid, 2003f). Also available through the Web site at http://www.stanfordbinet.com.

scriptive report with graphs and analyses of score differences can be generated, copied to a word processor, and edited by the examiner. One of the main advantages of computer scoring is that the conversion of raw scores is done rapidly and with complete accuracy, as compared to manually finding each of the conversion tables in the various test manuals. Also, all of the analyses of score differences can be calculated quickly without hand calculations or retrieval of critical values for significant differences. Differences within the SB5 would include those between IQ scores or among Factor Indexes, or among all 10 subtest scaled scores. In addition, differences between SB5 scores and scores on the WJ III Tests of Achievement (Woodcock et al., 2001b) are also programmed into the system. Thus, the calculation of ability-achievement discrepancies for assessment of learning disabilities can be done by the program and entered into a computerized report for the user. Some of the features of the program are listed in Rapid Reference 3.2.

🖎 TEST YOURSELF 🖎

1. **What are the mean and standard deviation of normative scaled scores for SB5 subtests?**

    (a) 10 and 3

    (b) 50 and 10

    (c) 100 and 15

    (d) 500 and 100

2. **Which of the supplemental scores is derived from the sum of two subtest scaled scores?**

    (a) Change-Sensitive Score

    (b) Extended IQ

    (c) Abbreviated Battery IQ

    (d) Nonverbal IQ

3. **What is/are credited as base points for the functional level testlets?**

    (a) Scores from any two items below the starting point

    (b) The number of incorrect scores below the starting level

    (c) The maximum scores (4 or 6) below the starting level

    (d) None of the above

4. **What is the typical number of functional levels that examinees are administered in Item Books 2 and 3?**

    (a) only 1

    (b) 2 or 3

    (c) 3 or 4

    (d) 5 or 6

5. **Which scores are used to establish age equivalents?**

    (a) Full Scale IQ

    (b) Extended IQ

    (c) Abbreviated Battery IQ

    (d) Change-Sensitive Scores

6. **How many Factor Index scores are there and how many subtests are used to calculate them?**

   (a) Two scores from 5 subtests each

   (b) Three scores from 3 subtests each

   (c) Four scores from 4 subtests each

   (d) Five scores from 2 subtests each

7. **What is the approximate CSS value for the average 2-year-old?**

   (a) 340

   (b) 430

   (c) 453

   (d) 480

8. **What are the two major criteria used to interpret the criterion-referenced CSS?**

9. **Who originally developed the metric used for CSSs?**

10. **What are the ranges of Extended IQ scores in the currently available tables?**

    (a) 40 to 70 and 130 to 160

    (b) 20 to 50 and 150 to 180

    (c) 20 to 39 and 161 to 199

    (d) 10 to 39 and 161 to 225

Answers: 1. a; 2. c; 3. c; 4. b; 5. d; 6. d; 7. b; 8. age and task difficulty; 9. Richard Woodcock; 10. d

Four

HOW TO INTERPRET THE SB5

THE SEVEN-STEP INTERPRETIVE STRATEGY[1]

Most interpretative methods for intelligence scales begin with the global (Full Scale) scores. However, due to the strength of the nonverbal sections of the SB5, we suggest using a seven-step method that first emphasizes the differences between nonverbal and verbal scores. Each of the seven steps is detailed in the following pages, with examples of their application and a case study to emphasize the key features of interpretation. An interpretive worksheet for the seven steps is included in Appendix A.

Step 1: Assumptions

The first assumption of professional assessment is that standardized instructions have been followed exactly. When examiners change standardized procedures, the use of normative interpretations are at risk. Changes in procedures may invalidate the normative comparison between the examinee's performance and those of peers in the standardization sample. Alternatively, something in the physical condition of the examinee (such as illness) or other factors during the testing session may affect the examinee's performance. For these reasons, the assump-

---

[1] The seven-step interpretive strategy is reproduced from the *Stanford-Binet Fifth Edition, Examiner's Manual* by Gale H. Roid, Ph.D., with permission of the publisher. Copyright © 2003 by The Riverside Publishing Company. All rights reserved.

tion of a valid and standardized assessment must be examined by all users before you proceed with interpretation.

For example, suppose an examinee has a significant orthopedic impairment and is unable to point accurately or to respond to test items by moving blocks and other materials. As outlined in Braden and Elliott (2003), modifications may be necessary (and perhaps required by ethical and legal guidelines) and can be applied to the SB5. However, modifications that change the standardized administration by providing extra time or extra assistance by the examiner may change the basic assumptions of testing. Significant modifications may invalidate the use of standard norm tables, and the conclusions of test interpretation must be adapted.

Another basic assumption is that a valid test administration was conducted. Several factors may invalidate a testing session. Sources of possible invalidity can be illness or extreme distractibility of the examinee, unexpected interruptions, spoiled subtests (those with fatal flaws such as terminating too early, missing test materials, or other unexpected accidents), and other unusual events that occur near the testing site. Thus, interpretation must be adjusted when the testing session is compromised, or, alternatively, the IQ scores can be corrected by using the prorated tables of sums of scaled scores (Roid, 2003c, p. 256). Any of these circumstances should be noted on the SB5 record form and in any reports generated to describe the results of testing.

Step 2: Background and Context

The ethnic, gender, religious, cultural, or other characteristics of the examinee's background may greatly affect test interpretation. Unlike Step 1, in which standardized procedures are considered, Step 2 is concerned with context effects of the examinee's prior background that may impact interpretation of SB5 results. To fully understand the implications of this step, a case study will be used to highlight important considerations.

Suppose you have been asked to give the SB5 to a high school student we will call Noor. She is 16 years 10 months old and is a native of Pakistan who immigrated to the United States two years ago with her parents, who were both college educated. Although she spoke English during the testing session, her native language is Urdu and she is enrolled in an English-as-second-language program in her high school, where she receives 4 hr per week of language instruction. She speaks Urdu with her parents and relatives at home. As with many people who have recently immigrated, she has not yet mastered all the subtleties of the English language. Noor provides an excellent example of how the

---

☰*Rapid Reference 4.1*

Suggestions and References for Evaluating Acculturation Level of Examinee

- Each ethnic, religious, or cultural group may have different acculturation issues.
- See Dana (1993) or Paniagua (1994) for an overview of issues.
- Many brief questionnaires have been developed for different ethnic groups.
  African American: see Landrine & Klonoff (1994) or Snowden & Hines (1999)
  Asian: see Gupta & Yick (2001) or Nguyen & van Eye (2002)
  Hispanic: see Marin (1992) or Marin & Gamba (1996)
  Native American: see Paniagua (1994)
- Interview questions similar to those in formal acculturation questionnaires include the following types of questions:
  How many years have you been in this country?
  Would you describe yourself as the first, second, or third generation since your family moved to this country?
  Which language is spoken at home more often?
  What types of English (or majority, American, etc.) social activities do you and your family participate in?
  How many of your visual (film, TV) or print (newspaper, magazine) materials at home are in English?
  Describe some of the cultural activities that you and your family have continued since moving to this country.

context of the examinee must be taken into account when interpreting the SB5. Rapid Reference 4.1 lists suggestions and references for evaluating an examinee's level of acculturation. For additional guidelines, see Appendix A, Step 2.

Examinees with unique cultural backgrounds or a history of recent immigration (like Noor) have a variety of levels of acculturation into Western society. *Acculturation* is the process of adapting to a new culture and involves various levels of acquiring or rejecting the behaviors and attitudes of the host culture (Dana, 1993). Therefore, examiners should be aware that acculturation status must be assessed and use interview techniques or other methods of discovering what levels and types of acculturation have been acquired by the examinee. In Noor's case, she appeared for testing speaking English and dressed in Western clothing, but the examiner quickly discovered that her home environment was still oriented to her Pakistani culture and language. For these reasons, the examiner was cautious about Noor's depth of English-language mastery and familiarity with standardized testing practices.

The context of the examinee may affect test-taking skills or attitudes toward testing. For example, suppose a 13-year-old boy was raised in a unique culture, such as that of one of the peoples of New Guinea, and

DON'T FORGET

Some clerical accuracies that contribute to appropriate test interpretation include the following:

- Follow directions on the SB5 record form for combining *base points* (credit for previous items in the sequence, prior to the starting point) with *earned points* (items actually attempted and found correct).

- Check the context and background of the examinee before interpreting score levels or differences, especially in regard to the nonverbal and verbal difference (e.g., when the examinee is a recent immigrant to North America).

- Check the difference between Nonverbal IQ and Verbal IQ for statistical significance and rarity in the normative population before interpreting the level of the Full Scale IQ.

the items in the SB5 are unfamiliar to him. He may be less familiar with tests and react to items in unusual ways. If the examiner notes any unusual responses, a lack of responding, or general confusion on the part of an examinee recently immigrated to a European, Australian, or North American country, he or she should carefully note the skills and attitudes displayed by the examinee. It should not be assumed that the examinee is familiar with test-taking behaviors. Assistance is provided by the teaching items (sample demonstration items at the beginning of SB5 sections), but this brief introduction to test-taking may not be sufficient in all cases.

Step 3: Nonverbal IQ Versus Verbal IQ

Nonverbal IQ should be compared to VIQ using the typical methods of examining the statistical significance of the difference and its rarity in the normative population (Sattler, 1988, 2002). Extensive tables for evaluating such score differences among IQ, Factor Index, and subtest scores of the SB5 were presented in the SB5 *Technical Manual* (Roid, 2003f) and included in the SB5 scoring software. Definitions of each of these domain scores are presented in Rapid Reference 4.2.

Consider the case study of Noor, introduced in Step 2. Table 4.1 shows the IQ, Factor Index, and subtest scaled scores for Noor. Her NVIQ was 97, 19 points higher than her VIQ of 78, a difference that is statistically significant and relatively rare in the normative sample. Significance and rarity are determined from published tables, and they specify that differences greater than 8 to 10 points (depending on the age of the examinee) are sufficient for statistical significance. Rarity of the difference (infrequency in the normative population) requires magnitudes of at least 14 points or greater to reach *clinical importance* (defined as differences that occur in less than 15% of the population). Thus, differences of 14 points or more are both statistically significant and clinically important (see Appendix A, Step 3). Any report of Noor's results

≋ Rapid Reference 4.2

Definitions of SB5 IQ Scores

Full Scale IQ (FSIQ) measures a complex of different abilities, including the ability to reason with both words and visual material, the ability to store and later retrieve and apply important knowledge, broad span of memory for both words and visual details, spatial-visualization ability, and the ability to solve novel problems with numbers and number concepts.

Nonverbal IQ (NVIQ) measures reasoning skills in solving picture-oriented, abstract problems; remembering facts and figures presented in visual displays; solving numerical problems shown in picture form; assembling visual puzzles; and remembering information presented in visual space, such as the block-tapping sequences. The NVIQ shows how an individual retrieves and manipulates information presented in printed or spoken words and sentences.

Verbal IQ (VIQ) measures general verbal reasoning ability—solving problems presented in printed or spoken words, sentences, or stories. VIQ reflects the examinee's ability to explain details and events with clarity, verbally justify her or his rationale for answers to problems, remember details of spoken words and sentences, and explain spatial relationships.

should highlight the statistical significance and clinical importance of her 19-point difference (NVIQ vs. VIQ) and mention her language and cultural context. Instead of placing more emphasis on the FSIQ (which was 87 for Noor), the examiner should stress that her NVIQ of 97 probably represents a lower bound of her cognitive potential because of her English-language difficulties.

Thus, the general rules for interpretation are (a) check for statistical and clinical significance of the NVIQ versus VIQ difference first and (b) interpret FSIQ when the difference is small and not noteworthy (either statistically or in terms of frequency). If the difference is noteworthy, examine the context of the case in greater detail, and if the context

Table 4.1 Score Summary Report From the SB5 Computer-Scoring Software: The Case of Noor

Examinee: Noor P
Date of Birth: 9/15/1987
Date of Testing: 11/20/2003
Age: 16 years 2 months
Sex: Female

Examiner: A Smith
Date of Report: 11/20/2003
School/Agency: Central
Grade/Occupation: 12th Grade, Student
ID: ELL05

IQ and Factor Index Score Results

	Sum of Scaled Scores	Standard Score	Percentile	95% Confidence Interval Score Range	95% Confidence Interval Percentile
IQ Scores					
Full Scale IQ (FSIQ)	81	87	19	83–91	13–27
Nonverbal IQ (NVIQ)	48	97	42	91–103	27–58
Verbal IQ (VIQ)	33	78	7	73–85	4–16
Abbreviated IQ (ABIQ)	15	85	16	78–94	7–34
Factor Index Scores					
Fluid Reasoning (FR)	17	91	27	84–100	14–50
Knowledge (KN)	11	74	4	68–84	2–14
Quantitative Reasoning (QR)	19	97	42	89–105	23–63
Visual-Spatial (VS)	13	79	8	73–89	4–23
Working Memory (WM)	21	103	58	95–111	37–77

Table 4.1 Continued

Subtest Scores						

	Scores				Scores		
Nonverbal	Raw	Scaled	%ile	**Verbal**	Raw	Scaled	%ile
Fluid Reasoning	29	12	75	Fluid Reasoning	13	5	5
Knowledge	19	8	25	Knowledge	27	3	1
Quantitative Reasoning	24	11	63	Quantitative Reasoning	17	8	25
Visual-Spatial	19	7	16	Visual-Spatial	18	6	9
Working Memory	22	10	50	Working Memory	22	11	63

Sources: Roid (2003d, 2003e). Adapted and reproduced from the *Stanford-Binet Fifth Edition, Interpretive Manual* by Gale H. Roid, Ph.D., with permission of the publisher. Copyright © 2003 by The Riverside Publishing Company. All rights reserved.

supports the existence of significant English-language deficits or other cultural influences that affect test performance, consider using either NVIQ or VIQ instead of FSIQ as a general measure.

Step 4: Full Scale IQ

The FSIQ provides the most global, summary index of general cognitive ability across the five cognitive factors measured by the SB5. It is also the most reliable index of all SB5 scores because it is based on all parts of the test and research shows it to be internally consistent (technically, at the .98 level on a scale from .00 to 1.00). Investigators of intelligence theory, such as Carroll (1993) and Gustafsson (1984), would say that FSIQ estimates the g (general ability) that is found underlying all the scores within typical cognitive test batteries. Brief definitions of Full Scale and the other IQ scores of the SB5 are presented in Rapid

Reference 4.2. Descriptive categories for various score ranges on Full Scale IQ are provided in Appendix A, Step 4, Table A.1.

Kaufman (1990) found, as other researchers have, that general ability (FSIQ) is highly related to the total number of grades of education completed, occupational level, and other criteria important to society. Although not perfectly predictive of future behavior, FSIQ is one of the strongest predictors of overall success in education and work among the psychological measuring tools available to researchers. Of course, no particular intelligence battery, the SB5 included, can measure all the attributes of people that lead to success in school, work, and life. Dimensions such as athletic ability, musical ability, creativity, daily living skills, and perseverance are examples of factors not measured by FSIQ on the SB5 (as with most published intelligence batteries). For these reasons, FSIQ plays an important part in test interpretation, but should *not* be used as the only criterion to evaluate someone's potential for success in life.

Also, experts caution that general ability, reflected in FSIQ, can be affected by many environmental factors that can either increase or de-

CAUTION

Avoid overinterpretation of SB5 results. The results of intellectual assessments such as the SB5 should never be interpreted in isolation. The examiner should consider the context of the evaluation, environmental conditions of testing, examinee behavior and moods during the administration, and possible disabilities and linguistic or cultural factors. In addition, the results can be interpreted with greater confidence when you include other assessment instruments that can bear upon the meaning of SB5 scores. These may include the clinical interview, emotional and personality assessments, academic achievement tests, memory and other neurological assessments, and assessment of malingering. The use of scores without good contextual understanding may lead to inappropriate and unethical decisions.

crease cognitive performance. For example, poverty or cultural depri-
vation, illness or accidental injury, and violence or abuse can decrease
the cognitive functioning in an individual, whereas wealth, health, and
a protected environment can promote cognitive growth. Also, on any
given day, the examinee may or may not show (or be able to show, due
to illness or emotions) her or his top potential, because all people have
bad days. For these and other reasons, FSIQ should never be presented
to the examinee, parents, guardians, teachers, or others as a static, life-
time, unchanging quality represented by a single number. Instead, all IQ
scores should be presented within a range of possible scores (the confidence interval shown in Fig. 4.1). This is true of all test scores, because
a degree of measurement error is present in all scores, but is particularly
important with FSIQ due to the high regard placed on intelligence in
Western society. As shown in Figure 4.1, the confidence interval is
asymmetrical around the examinee's score based on the recommenda-
tion of Dudek (1979). The interval is centered around the estimated

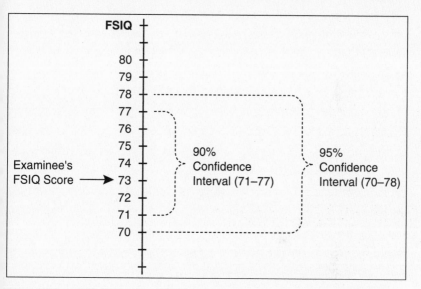

**Figure 4.1 Confidence intervals surrounding SB5 Full Scale IQ (FSIQ)
score of 73**

true score rather than the observed score. The true score is estimated to be closer to the mean (100) than the observed score.

Step 5: Factor Index Scores

Use the five Factor Index scores at the next level of interpretation, for several important reasons. First, the Factor Index scores are more reliable than individual subtest scores (in the .90 to .92 range, as compared to .84 to .89). Second, the Factor Index scores are based on extensive research in cognitive abilities (e.g., Carroll, 1993; Cattell, 1943; Horn & Cattell, 1966) spanning nearly 50 years. Third, the metric of these Factor Index scores is the typical standard score (with a mean of 100 and standard deviation of 15) used on many different tests; hence, ease of comparison across multiple tests. Fourth, the cognitive factors measured by the SB5 align with those of CHC theory (McGrew & Woodcock, 2001) and the cross-battery approach developed by McGrew and Flanagan (e.g., Flanagan & Ortiz, 2001; McGrew & Flanagan, 1998). In the cross-battery approach, individual subtests (or combinations of subtests that measure a single factor) can be administered from two or more cognitive test batteries and the results for a particular individual combined when making interpretations. Interpretations can be based on the standard definitions of each of the five cognitive factors given by Carroll and by McGrew and Flanagan, versions of which are provided in the text of the computer-scoring software for the SB5. For these reasons, the Factor Index scores of the SB5 provide the interpretive advantage of the long history of research and clinical practice over the last 50 years. Appendix B gives definitions and descriptions derived from Carroll's research on the cognitive components within each factor. Rapid Reference 4.3 provides definitions of the cognitive abilities measured by the SB5 Factor Index scores.

Plot the Factor Index scores for your examinee on the profile provided on the SB5 record form or obtain it automatically from the

≡ Rapid Reference 4.3

Definitions of SB5 Factor Index Scores

Fluid Reasoning (FR) is the ability to solve novel problems, whether presented in pictures and figures (nonverbal) or in words and sentences (verbal). FR includes both deductive (reasoning from principles) or inductive (discovering principles) abilities.

Knowledge (KN) is the accumulated fund of general information that a person acquires at home, school, work, and in daily life. Although it is highly related to educational attainment, it is more general than reading or academic skills learned in school. Instead, it includes understanding of the universe, natural laws, objects in nature, animals, people, facts, and concepts from everyday life.

Quantitative Reasoning (QR) is the ability to solve problems with numbers or numerical concepts. Although related to mathematics achievement, QR is the logical, reasoning aspect of understanding numerical and functional relationships. QR ability does not depend solely on the completion of certain academic mathematics courses or mastery of conventional mathematical procedures.

Visual-Spatial Processing (VS) is the ability to identify, analyze, and mentally rotate or assemble visual images, geometric shapes, or natural objects occurring in spatial arrangements. People skilled in VS can understand directions within a three-dimensional world and explain them to others. VS ability is often reflected in the work of architects, engineers, designers, artists, and other visually creative people.

Working Memory (WM) is the ability to store information in short-term memory and then sort or transform that information. Researchers have shown that there are two subsystems in WM: a visual-spatial "sketch pad" for visual information and a "phonological loop" for processing language and verbal information (Lezak, 1995, p. 29). These two subsystems are measured by the two SB5 subtests, one nonverbal and one verbal, that compose the WM Factor Index score.

scoring software. Look for distinct patterns of significant differences. As with all other SB5 scores, the magnitude of pairwise score differences can be compared to tables of statistical significance and frequency of differences within the normative population. Differences that are both significant (e.g., at the .05 level) and relatively rare in the population (e.g., occurring in less than 15% of the population) are clinically important and the focus of interpretation. Examiners should be cautious and not overinterpret small differences between Factor Index scores that do not meet the significance and frequency criteria.

In the case of Noor (Table 4.1), there are several pairs of Factor Index scores that have important differences. Noor's scores form an interesting **W** pattern, with FR (91), QR (97), and WM (103), all high within her profile, and KN (74) and VS (79), both quite low. There are four differences that are both statistically significant and infrequent in the normative population: the differences KN – QR (23), KN – WM (29), VS – QR (18), and VS – WM (24). Note that Noor's high scores of 91 to 103 are nearly average compared to the norm sample, so her high scores are relative strengths. Thus, Noor has relative strengths in the ability to reason with quantitative concepts and in the transformation of information in short-term memory (in both verbal and nonverbal ways). Her areas of relative weakness (KN and VS) are far below the national norm. Her score of 74 in Knowledge was due to her very low performance in Vocabulary (scaled score of 3), apparently because of her lack of knowledge of the definitions of a wide range of English words. As her English improves and her acculturation to the United States continues, this cognitive area should improve. In contrast, her score of 79 in Visual-Spatial Processing possibly reflects an area of cognition— the ability to analyze spatial relationships and geometric concepts— that may be a true weakness. However, even in the visual-spatial area, her subtest score of 6 on Verbal Visual-Spatial Processing is surprisingly low compared to other areas of her profile. This suggests that in-

DON'T FORGET

Interpretation of Differences Among SB5 Scores

IQ Scores

Look for differences of 14 points or more between Nonverbal and Verbal IQ before concluding that meaningful differences are present.

Factor Index Scores

Look for 18 or 19 (or more) points of difference between pairs of Factor Index scores before concluding that meaningful differences are in the profile.

Subtest Scaled Scores

First, calculate the average subtest score among the 10 subtests. Then, look for differences of more than 3 points between the individual subtest (the one that is higher or lower than average) and the average among all 10 subtests.

creased English competency may bring increased performance in expressing spatial concepts, giving directions, and so on.

Step 6: Subtest Comparisons

Some resources for interpreting SB5 subtest scores are provided in Appendix A (see Step 6) and Appendix B (see Tables B.2 to B.5). Table B.2 in Appendix B presents some of the cognitive components represented by the activities that compose the subtests within each cognitive factor. Table B.3 provides descriptions of the content of each of the 10 SB5 subtests. Table B.4 shows some of the cognitive abilities shared by combinations of SB5 subtests and the cognitive skills underlying performance on each subtest. Table B.5 provides expanded definitions of each of the cognitive abilities shown in Table B.4. Users can employ these tables in writing descriptive statements about the examinee's test performance in reports and summaries of SB5 results.

Clinicians have traditionally examined the subtest profile scores within one individual (called an *ipsative* comparison) for tests of cognitive ability. A few researchers have questioned the practice, however. McDermott, Fantuzzo, and Glutting (1990), for example, believed that most of the variation in individual subtest profiles of IQ tests was due to general ability (g). They showed the difficulty of identifying large numbers of profiles patterns in the normative data of various IQ measures, particularly the Wechsler scales. They used computerized cluster analysis to identify groups of examinees with similar profile patterns. They claimed that most of the profile patterns were flat (having all low or all high scores) rather than displaying scattered high and low scores. However, Roid (1994, 2003d) used the methods of Aldenderfer and Blashfield (1984) and showed that differentiated profile patterns can be found in 40% to 50% of individual profiles in large samples. The key to finding these differentiated profiles was to employ more-sensitive cluster analysis methods. Roid (1994) used Pearson product-moment correlations as the measure of profile similarity, rather than Euclidean distance. Aldenderfer and Blashfield (R. K. Blashfield, personal communication, February 22, 1992) recommended the use of Pearson correlations for the analysis of cognitive ability tests. This allowed interesting profiles to emerge more clearly in the normative sample of the SB5 (for example).

Another reason for clinicians to look for patterns among the subtest scores of the SB5 is the relatively high level of reliability of the scores compared to those of other cognitive batteries. The average internal consistency reliabilities of the SB5 subtests range from .84 to .89, which compares favorably to other batteries where subtests may have reliabilities in the .70 to .80 range. The error of measurement in one subtest is compounded when scores on two subtests are subtracted from one another (producing the difference that is the focus of any comparison).

Thus, the higher the reliability of subtests, the less error there is in the comparison of any two subtest scores and the less error in examining a pattern of several subtests. Reliability also affects a characteristic of subtest scores called *specificity*, which is discussed in the section on Advanced Subtest Interpretation (see Table 4.3).

Although caution is always recommended in interpreting profiles of scores, you can be confident in interpreting subtest

CAUTION

Always be cautious in interpreting individual subtest scores in isolation. Studying patterns of subtest scores can be helpful (see section on Core Profile Patterns From the Normative Sample), but overinterpretation of each subtest score individually should be avoided when results are inconsistent with other data such as interviews, observations, personality and other assessments, medical history, and parent reports.

patterns on the SB5, for the reasons stated previously. As with Factor Index scores, the two criteria used to interpret differences among the SB5 subtest scores are (a) statistical significance and (b) frequency of the difference in the normative population. However, instead of just comparing each pair of subtests, the most technically acceptable comparisons are between each subtest score and the average of all the individual's subtest scores. For example, take Noor's subtest scores from Table 4.1 and you will find a sum of 81 across the 10 subtest scaled scores, resulting in a profile average of 8.1 points. The largest and most significant differences from the 8.1 average are the high score of 12 on Nonverbal Fluid Reasoning and the low score of 3 on Verbal Knowledge. Each of these scores is more than 3½ points from the average of Noor's profile, indicating the presence of an important relative strength and an important relative weakness. This method of comparing scores to a profile average (see Rapid Reference 4.4) provides a built-in statistical control for the multiple paired comparisons being made between subtests. The method also provides a conservative approach to finding

≡Rapid Reference 4.4

Method of Comparing Subtest Scores to the Average of All Subtest Scores

The method of comparing scores to an individual's average score was originally developed by Davis (1959) and refined by Silverstein (1982). The minimum difference required for statistical significance is calculated using the *standard error of measurement (SEM)* of each subtest. These *SEM* values are relatively small for SB5 subtests, ranging from 1.01 to 1.22. First, all 10 of the squared values of the *SEMs* are summed together, resulting in a sum approximately equal to 12. This sum is divided by the number of subtests (10) squared (100), resulting in the decimal value 0.12. Next, the square of the individual subtest *SEM* (e.g., 1.18 for Nonverbal Fluid Reasoning [NVFR]) multiplied by a factor of .8 derived from the number of subtests (10 − 2 divided by 10) and added to the previous sum results in a total of about 1.235. The square root of this total is about 1.11, which is multiplied by the normal curve equivalent at the .05 level. However, this significance level is corrected by dividing it by the number of subtests, resulting in .005, to correct for multiple comparisons. The normal curve equivalent of a two-tailed test at the .005 level is 2.81, which is multiplied by the 1.11 value, resulting in the final value of about 3.09 (or, more precisely, 3.13, as listed in the official tables by Roid, 2003f). Therefore, the difference between the individual subtests (e.g., NVFR) in Noor's profile in Table 4.1 and the profile average must be greater than 3.1 to be used in interpretation. For a more detailed discussion and the actual formula, see Roid (p. 122).

strengths and weaknesses without overinterpreting small differences (see Appendix A, Step 6, worksheet).

The final step in comparing subtest scores would be to carefully compare large differences between the nonverbal and verbal pairs of subtests (e.g., Verbal vs. Nonverbal Knowledge). There are numerous neuropsychological implications of these differences. For example, the two Working Memory subtests were designed to measure the functioning of two different subsystems, or "sketch pads," in the brain, as described by Baddeley (1986). In the case of Noor (Table 4.1), large and significant differences are found between the Nonverbal and Verbal Fluid Reasoning subtests (12 vs. 5, a difference of 7 points) and the Nonverbal and Verbal Knowledge subtests (8 vs. 3, a difference of 5 points). In Noor's case, these differences are attributed to her English-language status more than to cognitive process differences.

Step 7: Qualitative Interpretation

Clinicians are very creative in developing ways of interpreting sequences of item responses, problem-solving styles, and various behavioral reactions to the testing situation. These creative explorations are part of a qualitative interpretation of the SB5 as contrasted to a score-based interpretation. The three main strategies suggested for qualitative interpretation of the SB5 are (a) using test-session behavior to temper interpretations of test scores, (b) testing the limits, so to speak, by retesting or interview procedures following the completion of standardized administration of the SB5, and (c) various interpretations specific to certain subtests. These strategies are discussed in a summary table provided in Appendix C.

Test-Session Behavior

Questions and space for notes on the behavior of the examinee during the test session are provided on page 2 of the SB5 record form. This includes concerns about the examinee's use of English language and his or her vision, understanding of directions, motor abilities, and general physical health during testing. Also, concerns include examinee cooperativeness, mood, activity level, attention and concentration, as well as the general validity of testing in terms of truly measuring the examinee's current level of functioning. When any of these concerns is severe, such as when there are significant vision problems, emotional reactions, illness, or extreme distractibility, be very cautious about interpreting SB5 scores. Instead, talk to parents, teachers, or caregivers, and consider rescheduling the testing for another occasion. When the behaviors are notable but not severe, include descriptions of them in any final report of SB5 score results.

Testing the Limits

Sometimes, clinicians return to certain tasks or items in a test after the standardized administration has been completed. They hypothesize that the examinee may be able to do some of the tasks in the test under different conditions than those specified by the standard administration instructions. For example, elderly examinees may be able to remember verbal material if it is repeated twice instead of just once (as required by the standard administration of Verbal Working Memory). Individuals with orthopedic disabilities may be able to assemble Form Patterns designs if they are assisted in moving the pieces. Examinees with attention deficits may be able to perform tasks if greater direction, assistance by the examiner, or additional prompting is given. Individuals with traumatic brain injury may be better at certain verbal tasks, but less good at visual-spatial tasks, suggesting more allowance of verbal explanation in nonverbal tasks. Some clinicians who are trained in "dynamic assessment" (Feuerstein, Rand, & Hoffman, 1979) may teach strategies of problem solving after an initial test administration to see if performance improves on a retesting (without repeating the actual items of the SB5, to avoid teaching to the test). Many of these procedures would be considered adaptations of the SB5; hence they would be done only after completion of a standardized administration, for purposes of comparison.

Additional Interpretations

Certain subtests or the activities within them can be interpreted in unique ways. For example, on the Vocabulary subtest, the examinee may have a pattern of incorrect responses on scientific words or words containing more than four syllables, or some other unique category of words. On the game of sorting picture chips in Verbal Fluid Reasoning, the examinee may have very creative categories, or, alternatively, may be stuck on color categories and not achieve the higher developmental concepts of functional categories (e.g., all the writing utensils). On Quantitative Reasoning, the examinee may do well on calculation problems, but less well on problems that involve geometric or measurement concepts. On any of the verbal subtests, articulation or expressive language oddities can be noted and relayed to a speech and language specialist. On nearly every subtest, the record form can be inspected to see if the examinee has a pattern of missing easy items while passing difficult items. Such an unexpected pattern may suggest that the examinee is distractible or otherwise diverted from the task on occasions. This may occur only on certain tasks, and the examiner needs to ask the examinee to explain how he or she felt about the problematic tasks. And, finally, there are many ways to experiment with testing conditions or conditions of the examinee, such as when children with hyperactivity are tested on two occasions—once with anti-hyperactivity medication and once without. Comparisons of results on two or more testing occasions may prompt other interesting clinical hypotheses and also allow use of the innovative Change-Sensitive Scores (CSSs; see Chap. 3).

ADVANCED SUBTEST INTERPRETATION

Several advanced methods of interpretation are used on the subtest profile scores of intelligence batteries. One is to consider the relationship between each subtest and the underlying general-ability factor (g), which helps in the anticipation of subtests that frequently differ from the remainder of the profile. Second is to consider the specificity (specific variance) of each subtest, which helps to evaluate and identify the subtests that have unique qualities not shared by the other subtests. Third is to consider the naturally occurring, core profile patterns that appear in the normative sample, which verifies that the test produces differentiated profiles characteristic of different cognitive styles. Each of these methods will be discussed in this chapter and additional methods of clinical interpretation will be discussed in Chapter 6.

General-Ability Factor Loadings

By knowing the general factor loading (g-loading) of each subtest in a battery, clinicians can anticipate which subtests may be consistent with or deviant from the overall level of functioning of the individual. In other words, a low g-loading can mean that a subtest will show more deviation from cognitive level indicated by the average of the individual's subtest scores. In the case of Noor (Table 4.1), her low score on the Nonverbal Visual-Spatial subtest is less surprising when you know that this subtest has slightly less g-loading than other SB5 subtests (see Table 4.2). There are several ways that researchers have estimated the g-loading of subtests. Kamphaus (1993) and Kaufman (1994) have used the first unrotated factor in principal components analysis to estimate the g-loadings of subtests on IQ tests. Kamphaus introduced one method of classifying the level of g-loadings using categories of *good, fair,* and *poor.* Subtests with g-loadings above .70 were considered good, those in the range of .50 to .69 were fair, and those below .50 were poor. The same classification and factoring method was used on the SB5 (Roid, 2003f) and the results are summarized in Table 4.2.

Nearly all the SB5 subtests are good measures of general ability, as shown in Table 4.2. The only exceptions are the Nonverbal Fluid Reasoning subtest in the 2–5 and 6–16 age ranges, and the Nonverbal Visual-Spatial subtest in the 2–5 age range. Practically, these results suggest that clinicians can count on each SB5 subtest to measure aspects of intellectual ability (e.g., as compared to aspects of cognitive skills less related to intellectual reasoning). Also, clinicians should not be surprised if Nonverbal Fluid Reasoning (Object Series/Matrices) scores or Nonverbal Visual-Spatial Processing (Form Board and Form Patterns) scores depart from the average subtest score for young children. As

Table 4.2 SB5 Subtest General-Factor (g) Loadings Considered Good or Fair, by Age Group

	Ages 2–5		Ages 6–16		Ages 17–85+	
	Good	Fair	Good	Fair	Good	Fair
Nonverbal						
Fluid Reasoning		.60		.69	.75	
Knowledge	.70		.78		.84	
Quantitative Reasoning	.79		.81		.83	
Visual-Spatial Processing		.65	.73		.79	
Working Memory	.72		.71		.77	
Verbal						
Fluid Reasoning	.75		.76		.80	
Knowledge	.75		.74		.75	
Quantitative Reasoning	.74		.82		.86	
Visual-Spatial Processing	.78		.81		.85	
Working Memory	.78		.72		.78	

Source: Tables adapted from Roid (2003f, p. 106). Reproduced from the *Stanford-Binet Fifth Edition, Technical Manual* by Gale H. Roid, Ph.D., with permission of the publisher. Copyright © 2003 by The Riverside Publishing Company. All rights reserved.

Note: Loadings are those of the subtest on the first unrotated principal component as derived from component analysis of the three age groups consisting of 1,400, 2,199, and 1,200 subjects, respectively.

expected from other research (e.g., Kaufman, 1990; Roid, Prifitera, & Weiss, 1993), the general factor plays a larger role in the adult age range, particularly above age 50 (Roid, 2003f). This trend seems to imply that intellectual abilities become more integrated and less scattered as people reach their elderly years. Clinicians should not be surprised to find more "flat" profiles (those with all subtests approximately the same) among the elderly, except for the well-known fact that memory abilities may show more decline than crystallized abilities (e.g., Vocabulary).

The findings in Table 4.2 are also important because they demonstrate the construct validity of the SB5 in relation to other editions and other IQ tests. In comparison to the fourth edition (SB4), many of the same subtests show very strong g-loadings. Nearly all the subtests of the SB4 that were retained in the SB5 (Vocabulary, Quantitative, Matrices, Absurdities, and Memory for Sentences) showed excellent g-loadings in the SB4 and again in the SB5. Subtests from the SB4 that were dropped in the SB5 included several with lower loadings (e.g., Bead Memory, with .68; Copying, with .61; Memory for Objects, with .54), according to the data in Sattler (1988). In addition, the SB5 compares favorably in overall average percentage of general-ability variance (the square of the average g-loading) to that of other tests. The square of the average g-loading on the SB5 (.78) is 61%, and this general-ability percentage compares well to the 50% found for the Wechsler Adult Intelligence Scale–Third Edition (Kaufman & Lichtenberger, 1999) and to the 39% found for the Wechsler Intelligence Scale for Children–Third Edition (Roid et al., 1993). The stronger g-variance of the SB5 is probably related to the nature of the items in the Stanford-Binet tradition—items that each measure combinations of complex mental abilities. SB5 Working Memory, for example, goes beyond short-term recall to the process of sorting or transforming information in short-term memory.

Before moving on to other advanced interpretive topics, the limitations of the g-factor should be mentioned. In modern society, the IQ score has taken on magical status, as if it were a fixed quantity that predicts great success in life with no error component. Clearly, those who know the limitations of any assessment device know that modern IQ tests have measurement error and do not include all the talents, skills, and abilities that could possibly be measured in individuals. Most IQ measures, including the SB5, do not include abilities such as artistic abilities, creativity, athletic prowess, or various social skills, including what has been called "emotional intelligence" (Goleman, 1995; Salovey & Mayer, 1990). Also, IQ measures are known to be related to the number of years of education, the educational and occupational levels of parents, and other demographic factors (Kaufman, 1990) that suggest strong environmental influences on IQ. With all these limitations and questions about general ability (IQ), caution should be taken in overemphasizing the g-loadings of SB5 subtests, as discussed previously.

Subtest Specificity

In contrast to general-factor variance, in which subtests share a common dimension, *subtest specificity* measures the degree of uniqueness in a subtest. Specificity is estimated from factor analysis and from the reliability of the subtest. First, the average internal consistency reliability of each subtest is subtracted from 1.0 to obtain the proportion of error variance, expressed as a percentage (e.g., for a subtest with .85 reliability, error variance is 1.0 minus .85 equaling .15, or 15%). Second, the common variance is obtained from factor analysis and is estimated from the communality of each subtest (amount of shared variance between the subtest and all the other nine subtests in the SB5) calculated on the normative sample at various age levels. The sum of the common variance and the error variance is subtracted from 100% to obtain the specific variance of the subtest. The average specific variance of each subtest, expressed as a percentage (specificity), is presented in Table 4.3, along with the error variance. The ideal pattern is to have specificity greater than 25% and error variance much lower. The average specificity across age groups, as shown in Table 4.3, is very representative of the more detailed findings presented by Roid and Pomplun (2004).

Following Kamphaus (1993), Table 4.3 shows specificity in three

Table 4.3 Percentages of Specific and Error Variance for SB5 Subtests at Three Age Levels

Subtests	Specificity Classification (%)		
	Ample	Adequate	Inadequate
Nonverbal			
Fluid Reasoning	33/15		
Knowledge		18/15	
Quantitative Reasoning			12/14
Visual-Spatial Processing	28/13		
Working Memory	30/12		
Verbal			
Fluid Reasoning		23/15	
Knowledge	28/11		
Quantitative Reasoning			14/13
Visual-Spatial Processing		17/13	
Working Memory	24/16		

Note: Variance percentages were derived from principal-axis factor analysis of the SB5 normative sample ($N = 4,800$), by permission of Riverside Publishing (Roid & Pomplun, 2004).

categories—*ample, adequate,* and *inadequate.* Only the Quantitative Reasoning subtests show specific variance nearly equal to error variance, the criteria for inadequate specificity. This occurs because of the high degree of common variance QR shares with all other subtests—73% to 74%, the highest in the SB5. Something about the complex reasoning in SB5 QR makes it quite central to the global factor in the SB5. However, while it is central to reasoning and global intellectual ability, QR sacrifices specific variation or uniqueness within the SB5. Thus, clinicians should be especially cautious not to interpret small differences between nonverbal or verbal QR and the other subtests. All the rest of the SB5 subtests have reasonable specificity, with Nonverbal Fluid Reasoning the best in the *ample* category (33% vs. 15% error variance), and Nonverbal Knowledge (18% vs. 15%) and Verbal Visual Spatial Processing (17% vs. 13%) the lowest within the *adequate* cate-

> # CAUTION
>
> Because of the low specificity of the Quantitative Reasoning subtests (due to their high common variance), avoid overinterpreting these individual scores in isolation from other data such as mathematics achievement, teacher ratings of math skills, and so forth.

gory. Detailed interpretations of the subtest scores of the five subtests in the *ample* category (Table 4.3) are encouraged because of their good patterns of specific variance combined with low error.

Core Profile Patterns From the Normative Sample

Another helpful analysis was conducted by Roid (2003d)—the derivation of core profile patterns from the SB5 standardization sample ($N = 4,800$). Core profiles are those that are typical because they occur with sufficient frequency (greater than 5%) in the normative population. Clinicians can use the knowledge of these core profiles to identify both common and unusual or unexpected profile patterns. Table 4.4 shows four common flat profiles and six differentiated profiles. In flat profiles, all subtest scaled scores are nearly the same, whereas in differentiated profiles, two or more subtests depart from the pattern of the others. Using Table 4.4, clinicians should compare the patterns of new examinees to those shown in the table to help identify common and unusual patterns. Furthermore, clinicians should be encouraged to use the SB5 subtest profile because, unlike the predictions of researchers such as McDermott and colleagues (1990), the profile scores are not so saturated with *g* that no unique patterns of scores are possible. As shown in Table 4.4, nearly half of SB5 normative profiles have identifiable pat-

Table 4.4 Core Profiles Derived From Cluster Analysis and Their Percentage in the SB5 Normative Sample

Name of Profile	Description of Score Pattern	Percentage
Flat		53
High ability	All scores near 13 or 14	9
Above average	All scores near 12	20
Below average	All scores near 8 or 9	13
Low ability	All scores near 5 or 6	11
Differentiated		47
High verbal ability	Nonverbal scores near 10, verbal near 12	6
High Quantitative	Both QR scores 12, all others near 10	8
High Fluid Reasoning	Both FR scores 11–12, all others near 10	9
High Knowledge	Both KN scores 12, all others 9–10	8
Low Fluid Reasoning	Both FR scores 8, all others 9–10	10
Low verbal ability	Nonverbal scores near 10, verbal near 8	7

Source: Adapted from Table 3.2 in Roid (2003d, p. 33). Reproduced from the *Stanford-Binet Fifth Edition, Interpretive Manual* by Gale H. Roid, Ph.D., with permission of the publisher. Copyright © 2003 by The Riverside Publishing Company. All rights reserved.

Notes: Based on analysis of 4,800 cases in the SB5 normative sample. Abbreviations are FR (Fluid Reasoning), KN (Knowledge), and QR (Quantitative Reasoning). All percentages rounded to the nearest whole number.

terns rather than a flat appearance predicted by heavy saturation of general-ability variance. Also, in clinical or referral cases, the presence of interesting patterns would seem to be more likely with the SB5 because of the patterns found in nonclinical, normative subjects.

SUMMARY

Many interesting and helpful strategies have been discussed for the interpretation of SB5 scores. An overall strategy involving seven steps of interpretation was presented and discussed in relationship to the interesting case of Noor, a recent immigrant to the United States from Pakistan. Many issues of language usage, acculturation, and score patterns were discussed and guidelines for practitioners presented. Details of the analysis of SB5 score differences were discussed, using the case study, showing how to employ statistical significance along with tables of the frequency of score differences in the normative population. Important differences are those that are both statistically significant and relatively rare in the population. Interesting qualitative interpretations, such as testing the examinee's limits of ability, are available with the wide array of subtest activities in the SB5. In addition, advanced methods of interpretation were presented, including analysis of general-factor loadings, specificity of subtests, and core profiles found in the normative sample. Additional techniques are also presented in Chapter 6.

 TEST YOURSELF

1. **Which is one of the primary issues addressed in Step 2 (Background and Context) of SB5 interpretation?**

   (a) Sensitivity to change and growth of young children

   (b) Whether the test was given in the standardized way and, thus, is a valid testing

   (c) The degree to which the examinee fits the cultural and linguistic expectations of SB5 testing

   (d) The magnitude of the differences between the average subtest score and an individual subtest score for all 10 subtests

   (continued)

2. **What type of scores are in the SB5 Factor Index profile, and what mean and standard deviation (SD) do they have?**

   (a) growth scores; mean 500, SD 9.1

   (b) standard scores; mean 100, SD 15

   (c) profile metrics; mean 50, SD 10

   (d) scaled scores; mean 10, SD 3

3. **What is the minimum size of the difference between an examinee's Nonverbal and Verbal IQ scores that would be considered meaningfully significant and unusual?**

   (a) 10 points

   (b) 14 points

   (c) 15 points (1 standard deviation)

   (d) 20 points (1.5 standard deviations)

4. **Which of the SB5 scores is an overall measure of g?**

   (a) FSIQ

   (b) NVIQ

   (c) VIQ

   (d) Verbal Knowledge

5. **Which of the SB5 subtests are highest in specificity?**

   (a) The two routing subtests, Nonverbal Visual-Spatial, and both Working Memory

   (b) The two routing subtests and Nonverbal Quantitative Reasoning

   (c) Vocabulary, Verbal Fluid Reasoning, and Nonverbal Quantitative Reasoning

   (d) Nonverbal Knowledge, both Visual-Spatial, and both Fluid Reasoning

6. **Which three SB5 subtests have the highest general-factor g-loadings?**

   (a) Nonverbal Fluid Reasoning

   (b) Nonverbal Knowledge

   (c) Nonverbal Quantitative Reasoning

   (d) Nonverbal Visual-Spatial Processing

   (e) Nonverbal Working Memory

   (f) Verbal Fluid Reasoning

   (g) Verbal Knowledge

   (h) Verbal Quantitative Reasoning

   (i) Verbal Visual-Spatial Processing

   (j) Verbal Working Memory

7. **What are the two criteria for evaluating score differences on the SB5?**

8. **Name two types of qualitative interpretation.**

9. **If the percentages of *common* variance and *error* variance for a subtest were 50% and 10%, respectively, what would the percentage of *specific* variance be?**

   (a) 80%

   (b) 60%

   (c) 50%

   (d) 40%

10. **Which core profile pattern had the highest percentage of occurrence in the SB5 normative sample?**

    (a) Flat profile, below average

    (b) Flat profile, above average

    (c) High Knowledge

    (d) Low Fluid Reasoning

Answers: 1. c; 2. b; 3. b; 4. a; 5. b; 6. c, h, i; 7. statistical significance and frequency; 8. test-session behavior; testing the limits; 9. d; 10. b

Five

STRENGTHS AND WEAKNESSES OF THE SB5

The fifth edition of the Stanford-Binet Intelligence Scales revived many of the classic features considered strengths in previous editions—toys for children, functional age levels, and expanded ranges of scores for low- and high-functioning examinees. At the same time, no psychological test is ever perfect, nor can a test provide all features needed by all possible test users. The SB5 was designed to meet the needs of educators and psychologists working with special education, preschool assessment, evaluation of individuals with mental retardation, gifted assessment, and other applications of previous editions of Stanford-Binet tests. A new emphasis was placed on assessment for adults and the elderly by extending the normative age range above 85 years. This emphasis had surprising benefits to school-aged assessment of learning disabilities by bringing increased attention to working memory, a highly effective predictor of learning difficulties, instead of traditional short-term memory. However, despite all the new features and benefits of the SB5, the test does not have all possible features for all possible assessment needs. Also, practical limits of cost and availability of clinical cases (e.g., the difficult-to-find cases of traumatic brain injury) prevented many of the extended research studies from being conducted during the time of SB5 development. These limits were extended by a massive development effort spanning 7 years, but even with this level of effort, published tests such as the SB5 always rely on future researchers to complete the extra studies needed for a full complement of clinical validity studies.

STRENGTHS AND WEAKNESSES OF SB5 DEVELOPMENT AND STANDARDIZATION

The SB5 has one of the larger standardization samples (4,800 subjects) among the published intelligence batteries, except the WJ III Tests of Cognitive Abilities (WJ III Cognitive; Woodcock et al., 2001b). And, as mentioned previously, the 7 years of development included numerous complex steps including pilot studies of new items and subtests, nationwide testing of a very comprehensive tryout edition, extensive normative data collection involving more than 500 examiners, and extensive reliability and validity studies. The age range of the SB5, from age 2 to above 85 (with the oldest subject being 96), exceeded that of any of the previous editions and is also somewhat unique for a cognitive battery, except, again for the WJ III Cognitive. The normative sample also shows excellent match to the ethnic and socioeconomic characteristics of the U.S. population (U.S. Census Bureau, 2001).

The SB5 was one of the first tests to undergo extensive fairness reviews by experts from various religious perspectives as well as those from representative ethnic, gender, and disability groups. Reviews of items, illustrations, and procedures were conducted by assessment professionals representing Buddhism, Christianity (both conservative and liberal denominations), Hinduism, Islam, and Judaism. Reviews were also conducted from the viewpoint of examinees with deafness and various disabilities. Ethnic perspectives were addressed by reviewers representing African American, Asian American or Pacific Islander, Hispanic American, and Native American or Alaskan Native populations. Reviews were conducted on both the tryout edition and the standardization edition of the SB5. These expert reviews were supplemented by extensive empirical studies of differential item functioning (DIF; Holland & Wainer, 1993) among the various gender and ethnic groups, using the Mantel-Haenszel statistical procedure (Holland & Thayer, 1988; Mantel & Haenszel, 1959). Rapid Reference 5.1 summa-

≡ *Rapid Reference 5.1*

Strengths and Weaknesses of SB5 Development and Standardization

Strengths	Weaknesses
Large norm sample ($N = 4800$)	Does not cover all of the possible factors in the CHC model
Extremely wide age range (2 to 85+ years)	More clinical and special group data needed
Norms fit 2000 census	More achievement test correlations needed
Extensive field testing and fairness reviews	
Content-validity studies of CHC-aligned factors	
Use of item response theory in development	
Linking of data with Woodcock-Johnson III Tests of Achievement	

rizes the strengths and weaknesses of the SB5's development and standardization process.

The SB5 items and subtests were also analyzed extensively using item response theory and Rasch item-calibration procedures (Rasch, 1980; Wright & Lineacre, 1999). This method allowed developers to construct the SB5 with several important features. First, the difficulty levels of all items and all testlets within each functional level could be calibrated with precision and related to previous calibrations of SB4 items. This allowed the SB5 to include items of known easiness or difficulty to extend both the low range and the high range of the test in comparison to the previous edition. Second, Rasch methods allowed the developers to effectively use the routing subtests (in Item Book 1) as an initial estimate of ability and to send the examinee to the appropriate functional level for the remainder of the test (e.g., into the level in Item Books 2 and 3 that matched the estimated ability score and the difficulty of the items located in that level). Finally, Rasch methods allowed for the development of the criterion-referenced Change-Sensitive Scores (CSSs), which provide an important supplementary scoring system (see Chap. 3).

Because intelligence batteries such as the SB5 are often administered along with achievement tests, a comprehensive linkage of the SB5 to the WJ III Tests of Achievement (Woodcock et al., 2001a) was also included in the standardization. A total of 472 students, ages 6 to 19, were administered the WJ III Achievement measures in reading, mathematics, and writing, along with the SB5. This provided the data needed to correlate the two batteries, as well as to document the distributions of ability-achievement discrepancies (see Chap. 6). Analysis of the WJ III measures is provided in the SB5 computer-scoring software (Roid, 2003e).

All of the SB5 features discussed to this point can be considered strengths of the battery because of the extensive nature of their development. However, there are inevitable weaknesses that should be noted. For users familiar with CHC theory and Carroll's (1993) factor studies, it will be obvious that not all possible cognitive factors were included for measurement in the SB5. A significant number (five) of CHC factors were covered—Fluid Reasoning, Knowledge (crystallized ability), Quantitative Reasoning, Visual-Spatial Processing, and Working Memory (short-term memory). However, one of the CHC factors not included in SB5 (but included in the Wechsler scales) is speed of processing. The typical subtests used to measure speed of processing have some of the lowest g-loadings among cognitive subtests (Kaufman, 1994), and thus were considered less central to the SB5's measurement of reasoning ability, the main focus of traditional Binet testing. Also, assessment professionals in special education and in giftedness education expressed concern that inclusion of speed of processing is sometimes unfair to children with cognitive exceptionalities. For example, many exceptional children are very meticulous or careful in solving tasks, and their latent ability can be underestimated when a test has a heavy saturation of speeded subtests or many time-bonus points. Other cognitive factors in CHC theory—auditory abilities and delayed-recall memory—were not included in the SB5. Measurement of these additional factors requires special equipment (e.g., tape recorders for auditory subtests) or difficult timing issues (e.g., careful timing of a 20-min delay for recall testing). Actually, the auditory, delayed-memory, and speed-of-processing factors were included in the early development of the SB5, but eliminated prior to the standardization due to the excessive length of the battery when these factors were included.

Final concerns about the development of the SB5 center on the limitations in covering all the possible disabilities (or subtypes, such as the varieties of learning disabilities) and all possible correlated tests in the SB5 validity studies. The SB5 included 1,365 subjects with exceptionalities or clinical diagnoses in its standardization studies, but even this large collection of subjects did not cover all possible special-education categories. No published test is developed with an unlimited budget, so the lack of extensive studies, especially of those involving the collection of longitudinal data over several years, is a weakness that can hardly be avoided in test development. Fortunately, for a test as well known as the Stanford-Binet,

DON'T FORGET

Two important changes in the Fifth Edition:

1. The standard deviation of SB5 IQ scores is now 15, not 16 as in all previous editions of the Stanford-Binet. This aligns the SB5 with virtually all other widely used tests and makes comparisons easier.

2. Optional new scoring with Change-Sensitive Scores (CSSs) promises great benefits for tracking improvement when examinees are tested multiple times across the years.

many independent researchers will conduct additional validity studies over the next decade, and users should watch for the emergence of publications on such studies.

STRENGTHS AND WEAKNESSES OF SB5 ADMINISTRATION AND SCORING

Strengths of the SB5 include the child- and examiner-friendliness of the new materials and procedures. Colorful toys, blocks, and illustrations help to engage children and also individuals with low cognitive functioning. The easel format of the item books and the design of the record form facilitate testing procedures for the examiner. The SB5 kit now includes a plastic tray with sections to hold the blocks, toys, and so on, making the materials easier to access during testing. The scoring system of the SB5 was revised to match the most common metrics in use by other cognitive tests—IQ scores with a mean of 100 and standard deviation of 15 (not the 16 used in prior editions) and subtest scaled scores with a mean of 10 and standard deviation of 3. The material and scoring improvements help make it easier for examiners to learn the new edition—a major concern among assessment professionals who feel challenged by the number of new test editions appearing in print.

The SB5 has several new innovations in scoring. First, the Rasch-based CSSs provide supplemental means of interpreting results. Because the CSSs are in a metric with equal numeric intervals and because they are anchored to age equivalents and to the difficulty of the items in the SB5, they form a criterion-referenced (Cohen & Swerdlik, 1999) scale. The values range from approximately 425 at age 2 years to about 525 at adult ages, with a center of 500 at age 10 years 0 months; hence, the criterion of age or developmental level underlies the scale. Except for a few other tests (e.g., the WJ III Cognitive by Woodcock et al., 2001b, or the Leiter-R by Roid & Miller, 1997), CSSs uniquely provide a method of interpreting change (e.g., growth) across multiple testing occasions.

The role of the supplemental CSSs takes on greater importance in the assessment of extremely low functioning or extremely gifted individuals. The conventional standard-score system, wherein scaled scores are summed to derive IQ scores, has an internal limitation on the range of final IQ scores—in the 40 to 160 range. This is because the scores are converted by a normal-curve transformation that restricts the range of scores at the extremes. Scaled scores of 1 and 19, for example, form arbitrary limits that merge all extreme cases at each end of the distribution. To prevent this restriction, the CSSs were used to derive an extended IQ (Roid, 2003d) that provides IQ values in the ranges of 10 to 39 and 161 to 225. The Extended IQ (EXIQ) is possible because the SB5 has some very easy and some very difficult items that allow the raw scores of the test to range very low and very high. The unusually wide range of extended IQ is possible because the CSS system and the resulting EXIQ is simply a transformation of raw scores. The only limitation to EXIQ is that tables are currently available only for the Full Scale IQ, not the Nonverbal or Verbal IQ or Factor Index scores.

Some examiners who are unfamiliar with the classic age-level design of the Stanford-Binet early editions have expressed concern about the functional levels in Item Books 2 and 3. Many examiners have years of testing experience with point scales in which each subtest

> # CAUTION
>
> Examiners who administer other intelligence tests may be tempted to administer each subtest separately in Item Books 2 and 3, assessing only one testlet per record-form page. Administering the SB5 in such a manner does not effectively save time or benefit the examinee. The standardized administration was thoroughly studied during the multiple years of developing the SB5 and provides advantages to the examinee. This format is a marked strength, providing streamlined administration and good cooperation while maintaining precise assessment.

forms a separate array of items that span the ages. Thus, examiners new to the SB5 have the urge to administer all the testlets across levels for each subtest to create point scales. However, field trials with the functional-level format of the SB5 showed that children were engaged and attentive to testing when there was variety at each age level (among the four testlets) as compared to the point-scale format used in the SB5 tryout edition. With the easel format of the item books, the plastic tray for access to materials, and clear directions, examiners use less effort in employing levels on the SB5 than they did historically on early Stanford-Binet editions.

> ### C A U T I O N
>
> Be aware that administration and scoring of Picture Absurdities requires some verbal dialogue. While these testlets do require brief spoken responses by the examinee, gestures and pointing are still allowed as supplements to brief vocalizations by the examinee. When interpreting Picture Absurdities scores (the Nonverbal Knowledge subtest), the thoughtful examiner will weigh issues other than spoken English—such as poor visual scanning abilities, performance anxiety, neurological damage, poor attention to detail, and so on—that may have affected the results.

Finally, another concern expressed by examiners is the definition of *nonverbal* in the SB5. Examiners familiar with nonverbal measures such as the UNIT (Bracken & McCallum, 1998) and the Leiter-R (Roid & Miller, 1997) will note that the SB5 uses some brief spoken directions by examiners. Other nonverbal measures use pure pantomime or gestures in the test directions. The long history of the Binet tests, however, has always been to consider the test as part of a clinical interview, which obviously involves speech by the examiner. Also, the name *nonverbal* is the most common term in assessment for tests that do not require vocal expressive language (e.g., English) by the examinee. A more accurate description for the nonverbal sections of the SB5 would be "the low-language-demand section" or "the limited-receptive-language-with-out-expressive-language section," but these terms, although accurate, are quite long and difficult to employ on the record form, in advertising, and in brief communications about the test. Also, years of experience with pantomime directions by the SB5 author and developers led to the conclusion that many examinees can be confused by the lack of speaking by the examiner, and children will often ask, "Why don't you say anything?" Thus, the practical solution was to construct the test with brief examiner prompts, requiring only a small degree of English receptive language (often supplemented by gestures), in the test directions of the nonverbal sections.

One further comment on the nonverbal nature of the SB5 centers on the Picture Absurdities activity within the Nonverbal Knowledge (NVKN) subtest. Early experiments by the SB5 author with purely pantomime versions of picture oddities revealed that some degree of expressive vocal explanation by the examinee was required occasionally to define the oddity. Moreover, Picture Absurdities has historically been found to have some elements of language development as a cognitive element (e.g., McGrew & Flanagan, 1998). Recent confirmatory factor analyses of the SB5 showed the NVKN to load effectively on the Knowledge factor along with its verbal counterpart, Vocabulary. Examiners who test examinees with limited English or a history of recent immigration to the United States should emphasize gestures when brief vocal speech seems required on Picture Absurdities. In extreme cases where vocal speech is impossible for the examinee, prorating of the Nonverbal IQ should be considered. In prorating, the NVKN would be considered spoiled, eliminated from the nonverbal sum of scaled scores, and the NVIQ corrected by using the prorating table in the *Examiner's Manual* (Roid, 2003c). Rapid Reference 5.2 summarizes the strengths and weaknesses of SB5 administration and scoring procedures.

Rapid Reference 5.2

**Strengths and Weaknesses of SB5
Administration and Scoring**

Strengths	Weaknesses
Tailoring of levels to the ability of the examinee	Some examiners see levels as initially confusing (lack of familiarity with Form L-M format)
Scoring metrics now align with those of other batteries	
Child friendliness of the test	Examiners have some difficulty in shifting test materials between testlets
Innovative new Change-Sensitive Scores using item-response-theory model	
Extended IQ: 10 to 40 and 160 to 225	Conventional scaled scores and IQs limit range to 40 and 160
Well-designed record form	Extended IQ for Full Scale IQ only
Helpful examiner pages in item books	Lack of pure pantomime administration in nonverbal subtests
Kit provides a plastic tray for toys and manipulatives	Computer-scoring software not included in kit
User-friendly computer-scoring program is optional	Nonverbal Knowledge (Picture Absurdities) may require a degree of expressive language

STRENGTHS AND WEAKNESSES OF SB5 RELIABILITY, VALIDITY, AND TECHNICAL PROPERTIES

Continuing the long tradition began by Terman (1916), the SB5 has many excellent technical properties in comparison to other psychological tests. The SB5 shows high reliability among the IQ and Factor Index scores (.90 to .98) and among the subtests (.84 to .89) as compared to other tests (see Chap. 4). Correlations in the .80 to .90 range with other IQ measures helped to verify the validity of the SB5 Full Scale IQ (Roid, 2003f). The five cognitive factors were shown to be related to other measures of the CHC factors in a cross-battery factor analysis of the SB5 and the WJ III Cognitive scales, verifying the theoretical basis of the factor design. The new CSS scales were shown to demonstrate across-age trends similar to expected growth curves found on other tests such as the WJ III Cognitive and Leiter-R. Further research on CSSs may show the promise of these scores for mapping the development of cognitive abilities across the age range. Rapid Reference 5.3

═Rapid Reference 5.3

Strengths and Weaknesses of SB5 Reliability, Validity, and Technical Properties

Strengths	Weaknesses
Excellent subtest reliability (averages all above .84) and good specificity for most subtests allows reliable profile analysis	More concurrent correlations with other tests needed
High concurrent correlations with the SB4 and other IQ measures, as well as with achievement measures	Exploratory factor analyses may not agree with confirmatory results due to high g-loadings and subtest characteristics (e.g., the verbal loading on Picture Absurdities)
Good consistency of confirmatory factor analyses across age levels	Specificity of the Quantitative Reasoning subtests is very low
Cross-battery confirmation with Woodcock-Johnson III Tests of Cognitive Abilities validates Cattell-Horn-Carroll (CHC) factors	
Practice effect for nonverbal subtests is lower than with other batteries	

summarizes the strengths and weaknesses of the SB5's reliability, validity, and technical properties.

A surprising strength of the SB5 was identified by the test-retest reliability studies reported in Roid (2003f). The practice effects (measured by the score difference between initial and repeated testing) on the SB5 were smaller than expected. In comparison to the Performance IQ of the WISC-III (Wechsler, 1991) or WAIS-III (Wechsler, 1997), for example, the nonverbal IQ of the SB5 showed shifts of only 2 to 5 IQ points, instead of the 4 to 13 points on the Wechsler scales. The lower shift, and thus the practice effect, for the SB5 is even more notable given the shorter retest period (5 to 8 days for the SB5 vs. 23 to 35 days on average for Wechsler scales). Research usually shows that the shorter the retest period the greater the practice effect because the examinee remembers the details of the test items and directions in the shorter time period. The implications of the lower practice effect on the SB5 is that retesting can be done earlier on the SB5 than on other IQ batteries, perhaps as soon as 6 months rather than the typical 1-year delay.

In terms of technical properties, there are a couple of concerns that affect test interpretation on the SB5. First, the specific variance of the Quantitative Reasoning subtests is low (see Chap. 4), meaning that interpretations of individual varia-

---

DON'T FORGET

The high stability of SB5 IQ scores and their low practice effect allows retesting to be scheduled every 6 months rather than at the typical one-year (or longer) recommended time period.

CAUTION

Although performance on the Quantitative Reasoning (QR) subtests is highly related to overall ability (e.g., Full Scale IQ), the specific variance of QR subtests is low. This means that examiners should avoid interpreting these two subtests in total isolation of other information (e.g., math achievement, observations by math teachers).

tions in those subtests should be done cautiously because they are so highly related to the underlying general-ability factor of the SB5. Second, the slightly verbal nature of Picture Absurdities, as discussed previously, should be kept in mind when interpreting low scores on NVKN by adolescents with language backgrounds other than English.

STRENGTHS AND WEAKNESSES OF SB5 INTERPRETATION AND APPLICATION

Several new interpretive features were added to the SB5 to enhance the usefulness of the test in the diagnosis of academic difficulties, developmental delays in children, memory problems in the elderly, and the documentation of improvements in students enrolled in special education. These new features have been the focus of a comprehensive series of training workshops for the SB5 given in many cities of the United States (contact Riverside Publishing for further information). Changes from the memory subtests of the Fourth Edition to the Working Memory subtests of the SB5 added major interpretive advantages for several clinical conditions in both children and adults. The design of both nonverbal and verbal subtests to measure each of five cognitive factors also adds greatly to the clinical usefulness of the battery. The supplemental CSS scales add tools for measuring growth and responsiveness to intervention in students enrolled in special education, particularly those who typically score in the lower percentiles of normative scores. For these low-functioning, special students, parents and educators are often frustrated by an apparent lack of improvement, caused in part by the nature of normative IQ and scaled scores. These normative scores compare the student to age peers who are growing at a more rapid rate, resulting in the special student's appearing to remain at the same low level year after year. The CSS system is more sensitive to change than normative scoring systems, and even one additional raw score point will result in an increase in the CSS metric. CSS results collected across repeated years show promise for documentation of gains in special education, both for individuals and possibly for interventions or programs. Documentation of these results can be facilitated by the computer-scoring software for the SB5 (Roid, 2003e), which is distributed separately from the standard SB5 kit at additional cost. Rapid Reference 5.4

≡ Rapid Reference 5.4

Strengths and Weaknesses of SB5 Interpretation and Application

Strengths	Weaknesses
Working Memory enhances diagnoses	Nonverbal subtests require some degree of receptive language ability, as well as expressive ability on Picture Absurdities
Valuable contrasts between nonverbal and verbal subtests possible	
Comprehensive *Interpretive Manual* provided	Extra cost of *Interpretive Manual* and computer-scoring reports
Supplemental criterion-referenced Change-Sensitive Scores useful for documenting progress	More studies of classroom applications needed
Working Memory, Knowledge, and Quantitative Reasoning have promise for early prediction of learning disabilities	
Extensive series of training seminars provided	
Special Extended IQ with tables made for gifted assessment and low-mental-retardation cases	
New composite scores developed for early prediction of learning disabilities	

CAUTION

As is true of all intelligence batteries, subtests or composite scores of the SB5 are *not* perfect predictors of learning disabilities. SB5 scores should not be used in isolation to diagnose learning disabilities. Evidence from parents, teachers, achievement tests, and classroom observations should be used to supplement test data.

lists the strengths and weaknesses of SB5 interpretation and application.

As discussed in Chapter 6, the SB5 was designed to allow for the prediction of early emerging learning disabilities (LDs). Research has shown that several composites consisting of the Knowledge, Quantitative Reasoning, and Working Memory scores may begin to predict symptoms of LD as early as 4 years of age. The composite scores are not perfectly predictive and do not diagnose LD, of course, but may be used as screening devices. The advantage of their use is that they do not require the conventional discrepancy model, employing achievement tests in combination with the SB5. This is an advantage because it is difficult to measure true academic achievement, particularly in reading, prior to the second or third grade. Some of this research was reported in the *Interpretive Manual* (Roid, 2003d), which must be purchased separately from the standard SB5 kit.

As with nearly all published cognitive tests, and despite the many validity studies conducted for the SB5, details of the relationship between SB5 scores and the performance of children in school have not yet emerged. Independent researchers working in school settings are encouraged to conduct studies of the effectiveness of different teaching methods for students with specific SB5 profile patterns. Roid (2003f) has shown that the SB5 has strong correlations with achievement, but some of the details have yet to be documented.

🖎 TEST YOURSELF 🖎

1. **The SB5 composite scores do not diagnose learning disabilities, but may be very useful as screening instruments.** True or False?

2. **Which nonverbal subtest may require a small degree of spoken response by the examinee?**

    (a) Nonverbal Fluid Reasoning

    (b) Nonverbal Knowledge

    (c) Nonverbal Quantitative Reasoning

    (d) Nonverbal Working Memory

3. **Which of the following is *not* one of the strengths of the SB5?**

    (a) Very good subtest reliability

    (b) Wide age range, from 2 to above 85

    (c) Routing subtests used to tailor the test to examinee's ability level

    (d) Ability to complete comprehensive administrations within 15 min

4. **The SB5 was one of the first tests to employ fairness reviewers from religious perspectives.** True or False?

5. **Which of the following cognitive factors from CHC theory were not included in the final version of the SB5?**

    (a) Crystallized ability

    (b) Visual-Spatial Processing

    (c) Speed of processing

    (d) Fluid Reasoning

6. **A transformation of Change-Sensitive Scores (CSSs) provides a means of assessing extremely low but not extremely high IQ scores.** True or False?

7. **Name one of the primary advantages to the supplemental CSSs.**

8. **Which feature of the SB5 is a concern for examiners who have only used tests with a point-scale format?**

    (a) Extended IQ

    (b) Change-Sensitive Scores

    (c) Measuring of five cognitive factors

    (d) Subtests arrayed in a functional age-level design

(continued)

9. **What is the new standard deviation of IQ scores on the SB5?**

10. **What is the magnitude of the SB5 nonverbal IQ retest practice effect (the shift in IQ from test to retest)?**

    (a) 2 to 5 points

    (b) 4 to 8 points

    (c) 4 to 13 points

    (d) 5 to 15 points

Answers: 1. True; 2. b; 3. d; 4. True; 5. c; 6. False; 7. measuring change; 8. d; 9. $SD = 15$; 10. a

Six

CLINICAL APPLICATIONS OF THE SB5

This chapter presents ideas and methods for applying the SB5 to clinical and exceptional cases, diagnostic hypotheses, the assessment of various disabilities, and other clinical applications. SB5 research on the assessment and identification of learning disabilities provides examiners with several important resources and methods described in this chapter. For other applications, examiners often use combinations of subtests, called "shared ability" composites (Kaufman, 1994, p. 273) and this chapter presents some new composites recently developed by the SB5 author, along with brief guidelines for some other clinical applications such as forensic evaluation and assessment of traumatic brain injury. Because of the large array of possible clinical applications of tests like the SB5, only a few can be covered here. The reader should watch for future publications and research papers that will emerge in the literature on the SB5 for additional clinical applications.

ASSESSMENT OF LEARNING DISABILITIES

The President's Commission on Excellence in Special Education (2002) conducted a comprehensive review of the process of identifying learning disabilities (LDs) in U.S. schools. Currently, many practitioners do not know the full implications of the reauthorization of the Individuals with Disabilities Education Act (IDEA, 1997) and implementation of any new regulations in each local or state education agency. However, initial testimonies in Congress by experts (e.g., Stuebing, Fletcher, LeDoux, Lyon, Shaywitz, & Shaywitz, 2002; Torgesen, 2002) criticized the traditional method of calculating the difference between ability (IQ scores) and achievement. Experts were concerned that conventional IQ-discrepancy methods were not sensitive to early-emerging LD because reading comprehension is not fully developed until elementary school (Aaron, 1997). Also, IQ-discrepancy methods are weak in identifying slow learners—those who are low on both ability and achievement (Stuebing et al.). Because of these concerns, SB5 users should watch for possible changes or additions to regulations on LD identification that may be adopted by their local and state education agencies.

Regardless of changes in LD regulations, the SB5 provides the user with several alternatives for assessing LDs—early-prediction formulas, research on the scores of slow learners, and two approaches to IQ-discrepancy analysis. This chapter briefly describes each alternative and provides useful tables for implementing these approaches.

Early Prediction of Learning Disability

Evans, Floyd, McGrew, and Leforgee (2001) showed that cognitive ability scores based on the CHC model can be very effective in early prediction of reading, mathematic, and other academic underachievement. Given that the SB5 measures some of the key abilities, such as Knowledge and Working Memory, that are predictive of learning difficulties, SB5 scores can be used in the early age range for prediction of LD. Research by Roid (2003d) and Roid and Pomplun (2004) showed that SB5 Working Memory and Knowledge scores were predictive of reading achievement and Working Memory and Quantitative Reasoning predictive of mathematics achievement. This research promises to provide a method of predicting risk for LD with the SB5 alone, instead of waiting for reading skills to develop in elementary school when achievement tests can be given.

As shown in Table 6.1, composite scores can be calculated from SB5 subtest scores to predict the risk of LD in the age range of 5 to 7 years and beyond. Tellegen and Briggs (1967) origi-

> # CAUTION
>
> Examiners should use the composite scores shown in Tables 6.1 and 6.2 for either screening purposes (with subsequent extended assessment or referral) or generating clinical hypotheses to use in writing test reports *only*—not for diagnosis.

nated the idea of combining subtest scores to form composites for the Wechsler scales, and many more composites have since been developed (e.g., Kaufman, 1994). Roid (2003d) showed that the LD–Reading composite in the upper section of Table 6.1 (the sum of NKN, VKN, NWM, and VWM subtest scaled scores) identified 66.7% of cases with documented disabilities in reading. A total of 528 cases in the 5- to 7-year-old age range, including 27 with document reading disabilities, were classified using a cut-point of 89 points on the new composite standard-score scale (see the equation in Table 6.1) with 81% of cases classified correctly overall. Documented LD cases had been established by independent assessment in schools using IQ measures other than the SB5 and achievement tests to verify the presence of LD. The reliability of the composites in Table 6.1 (.95) is quite high because the reliabilities of the four subtests (.84 to .89) combine. However, examiners should use this composite for screening purposes, not diagnosis, because the classification is adequate only for identifying risk status. For example, the LD–Reading composite, with a cut-point of 89, still identifies *false-positive* cases (those that are actually normative cases, erroneously labeled LD) at a 17% rate.

To calculate the composites, use the example in Rapid Reference 6.1 as a guide. Add the four subtest scaled scores together to form the sum, then multiply the sum by the value indicated in the equation and add the

Table 6.1 Learning-Disability Composites of SB5 Subtest Scaled Scores: Formula for Sums, Reliability and Conversion Equations

Composite	Formula for Sum	Reliability	Equation
Early Learning Disabilities (Ages 5–7)			
LD–Reading	NKN + NWM + VKN + VWM	.95	1.875(Sum) + 25.0
LD–Mathematics	NQR + NWM + VQR + VWM	.95	1.875(Sum) + 25.0
School-Age and Adult Learning Disability			
LD–Reading	NKN + NWM + VKN + VWM	.95	1.56(Sum) + 37.9
LD–Mathematics	NKN + NWM + VKN + VWM	.95	1.49(Sum) + 41.2

Notes: Abbreviations are LD for learning disability, N for Nonverbal, V for Verbal, KN for Knowledge, QR for Quantitative Reasoning, WM for Working Memory, and Sum for the sum of the scaled scores of the subtests in the composite.

≡ *Rapid Reference 6.1*

Example of the LD–Reading Composite Score Calculation for a Young Boy With Documented Learning Disability in Reading

Subtest Name Included in Composite	Scaled Score and Sum
Nonverbal Knowledge	7
Nonverbal Working Memory	4
Verbal Knowledge	4
Verbal Working Memory	5
Sum of Scaled Scores	20
Example of Equation and Calculation Results	
Step 1: 1.875 (Sum)	1.875 (20) = 37.5
Step 2: Add 25.0	37.5 + 25.0 = 62.5
Step 3: Round off the result	63

final constant to the result. The case shown in Rapid Reference 6.1 has a composite score of 63, which is quite low compared to a mean of 100—more than 2 standard deviations below average, giving a strong indication of risk for LD in reading. Of course, the case was selected as an example, knowing that this boy had been previously identified with LD by a local school district. Note that the equation changes slightly for screening of LD in the school-aged range (6 to 18 years) and above. If the boy had been older, the resulting value would have been 69, still more than 2 standard deviations below the average of 100. The LD composites in the lower section of Table 6.1 were recalculated on the SB5 normative sample for older examinees. Because the standard deviation of the composite is different in older examinees, the equation has slightly different

CAUTION

Be cautious in evaluating the SB5 scores of slow learners (Full Scale IQ 71 to 85). Discrepancies between IQ and achievement are rare and smaller than for other learning-disabled students—in the 10 point range. Consider learning disability (LD) risk only for such cases when other indicators of LD are present, such as low Working Memory scores or scores from other LD instruments or data.

constants than those in the early-prediction equations in the upper section of Table 6.1, as derived by Roid (2003d).

Slow-Learner Profile

When teachers identify students having difficulty in classroom learning, the students are often slow learners and do not, strictly speaking, have LD by current definitions of IQ discrepancy. These students often score in the range of 71 to 85 IQ, and thus show few significant discrepancies between IQ and achievement because both types of scores are low. Roid (2003d) found that discrepancies of about 10 points (smaller than the typical 20-point discrepancies found in LD identification) were found in about 3% of slow learners in a special sample. The special sample consisted of 99 students, aged 5 to 18, given both the SB5 and the WJ III Achievement (Woodcock et al., 2001a). WJ III Achievement scores were subtracted from the SB5 Full Scale IQ to calculate the discrepancies. Based on this somewhat small sample, examiners should look for discrepancies of lower magnitude—in the 10-point rather than the 20-point range—with caution. The search for these small discrepancies should be done only when there are additional indicators of LD risk, especially low subtest scores on the Working Memory, Knowledge, and Quantitative Reasoning subtests (both nonverbal and verbal) as found in research on the prediction of LD (Roid, 2003d). Examiners should note a tendency for slow learners to have their lowest scores on the Verbal Fluid Reasoning and Verbal Quantitative Reasoning subtests as compared to the remaining eight subtests (Roid).

Predictive Method of IQ Discrepancy Analysis

For many years, the calculation of discrepancies between IQ and achievement scores has been the main method of identifying LD. Shepard (1980) and many researchers that followed her lead (e.g., Braden & Weiss, 1988; Kavale & Forness, 1995) demonstrated the superior psychometric properties of the predictive method. In this method, IQ scores are correlated with achievement scores in a research sample who are given both IQ and achievement tests. The resulting correlations are used to produce a table of predicted achievement using a regression equation. This predictive method takes into account the correlative relationship, error of measurement in the two scores, and corrects for under- or overprediction bias that may be present in the simple subtraction of the two scores (Braden, 1987).

Start the predictive method by administering the SB5 with an achievement test such as the WJ III Tests of Achievement (Woodcock et al., 2001b). Suppose you find a discrepancy between the SB5 Full Scale IQ and the Reading Comprehension cluster score of the WJ III Achievement. Traditionally, you use two criteria for evaluating the size of the discrepancy—statistical significance and frequency in the normative population. Computer programs (e.g., Roid, 2003e) typically evaluate both these criteria automatically. To begin this evaluation by hand, find the predicted achievement value using tables of IQ prediction in Roid (2003f). The tables are based on the correlations between the SB5 and the WJ III Achievement, with Reading Comprehension correlated .75 with FSIQ, for example. As shown in Rapid Reference 6.2, suppose the 11-year-old student you have tested gets a standard score of 90 on Reading Comprehension and 110 on the SB5 FSIQ. You use the correlation of .75 and the formulas in Rapid Reference 6.2 to calculate a predicted achievement score (111 in this case). The predicted achievement score is always closer to the mean (100) than the original score, by nature of the regression method. Now, you subtract the actual achievement score (90)

≋ Rapid Reference 6.2

Example of the Predictive Method of Identifying Discrepancy Between WJ III Reading Comprehension (RC) and SB5 Full Scale IQ for an 11-Year-Old Student

Step in Calculation of Discrepancy	Formula	Result
WJ III RC = 90, SB5 FSIQ=115 (with correlation =.75)		
Step 1: Calculate Ability z score (Z)	$Z = IQ - 100$ divided by 15	= 1.00
Step 2: Multiply by correlation (r) to obtain regressed Z (RZ)	$RZ = r \cdot Z$	= 0.75
Step 3: Calculate predicted achievement (PRED), rounded to whole number	$PRED = 15 \cdot RZ + 100$	= 111
Step 4: Subtract actual achievement (Ach) from Predicted (PRED) to obtain discrepancy (DIS)	$DIS = PRED - Ach$	= 21

Evaluate results using Roid (2003f)	Table Value	Result
Step 1: Statistical Significance	11.38 (.01 level)	Significant
Step 2: Frequency	2% of population	Rare

from the predicted achievement (111 minus 90) and obtain the discrepancy of 21. As shown in the example, a 21-point discrepancy is both statistically significant (beyond the .01 level) and infrequent in the normative population, as determined from appendix C of Roid (2003d). Compare the frequency (2%) to the traditional clinical standard of 15% or less and conclude that this discrepancy is rare in the

> **CAUTION**
>
> Be cautious in evaluating the simple difference between SB5 IQ scores and achievement standard scores for purposes of learning-disability identification. Both scores have error of measurement that is multiplied in the simple difference. Also, Braden (1987) showed that the simple-difference method had more statistical bias across ethnic groups.

population. Therefore, you report that this case has a highly significant and clinically meaningful discrepancy indicative of a possible LD. Of course, you first present this evidence in a meeting with parents, a teacher, an administrator, and so on (those officially designated to attend a meeting in your school on the individual education plan [IEP] for the student), and the IEP group decides on the classification.

Simple-Difference Method of IQ Discrepancy Analysis

Some local and state agencies have regulations for LD identification based on the simple subtraction of IQ and achievement scores (Ross, 1995), known as the *simple-difference* method. Compared to the predictive method, the simple-difference method is quite easy. Simply subtract the achievement standard score from the IQ score. For the case in Rapid Reference 6.2, the discrepancy is 25 points. Tables in Roid (2003d), appendix D, show that 25-point discrepancies are both highly significant (less than .01) and highly infrequent (1%) in the normative population, again indicating the presence of a possible LD. Examiners should be cautious in using this method because it does not account for the measurement error that is multiplied when the two scores are simply subtracted.

OTHER CLINICAL APPLICATIONS

Instruments such as the SB5 have wide application in many clinical settings because of the wide age range of the normative sample (ages 2 to 85+) and the importance of measuring general cognitive ability. Professionals working in school settings probably conduct the greatest number of assessments with the SB5 because of its use in special education and school psychological services. However, developmental specialists in children's hospitals and preschool-assessment programs also apply the SB5 to evaluations of children aged 2 to 5 years. Clinicians working with adults and the elderly conduct evaluations for Workers Compensation and disability determinations as well as assessments of the effects of injury, illness, and aging. A few of these clinical applications are highlighted here.

DON'T FORGET

Be sure that scaled scores, not raw scores, are used in the shared composites. Scaled scores are the profile scales that range from 1 to 19 with a mean of 10 and standard deviation of 3.

General Clinical Applications: Shared Ability Composites

Expanding on the method developed by Tellegen and Briggs (1967), a series of "shared ability composites" (Kaufman, 1994, p. 273) was developed for general clinical applications of the SB5 (Roid, 2003a).[1] These composites are formed by summing sets of SB5 subtest scores. These sets of subtest scores share common characteristics—such as time limits, long questions, and so on—that require similar cognitive abilities, as defined in Table 6.2. When composite scores are either

---

[1] This section adapted from Roid (2003a). Reproduced from the *Stanford-Binet Fifth Edition, Assessment Service Bulletin Number 4* by Gale H. Roid, Ph.D. and Andrew D. Carson, Ph.D., with permission of the publisher. Copyright © 2004 by The Riverside Publishing Company. All rights reserved.

Table 6.2 Definitions of Shared Abilities Used in Composites Among SB5 Subtests

Composite	Definition
Planning Ability	The cognitive ability to recall and apply mental strategies for solving problems or completing tasks in an efficient manner.
Trial-and-Error Problem Solving	The mental strategy of trying multiple methods of solving problems, sometimes in a random order or fashion, until a solution is found.
Visual-Motor Ability	The neuropsychological processing and application of visual input to guide purposeful movements of body parts.
Abstract Conceptualization	Using principles, rules, and other concepts that generalize beyond a given task or setting to solve problems, reason, or form categories of information.
Understanding Long Questions	The ability to process all information in a long series of words or illustrations to understand the statement of a problem or question.
Attention and Concentration	Several mental and sensory processes that receive stimuli and focus the organism onto an array of incoming information. Includes selective attention, sustained attention (vigilance), divided attention, and alternating attention (Lezak, 1995).
Performance Under Time Pressure	Ability to remain focused on a task and continue to pursue solutions and remember details under time pressure.
High Performers Under Time Pressure	Ability to find solutions to difficult problems under time constraints. (*Note:* Use this composite only for examinees who reach Level 4 in Item Books 2 or 3.)

(continued)

Table 6.2 Continued

Composite	Definition
Cultural Knowledge	Ability to accumulate, recall, and apply factual and conceptual knowledge gathered from society, media, and everyday cultural experiences.
Acquired Knowledge	Accumulation, recall, and application of knowledge gained from formal schooling, training, or disciplined study.
Intellectual Giftedness	High levels of nonverbal problem solving and verbal reasoning in untimed tasks; excludes short-term memory. (*Note:* Use this composite for the highly verbal and meticulous examinee who is referred for gifted evaluation.)

Source: Reproduced from the *Stanford-Binet Fifth Edition, Assessment Service Bulletin Number 4* by Gale H. Roid, Ph.D. and Andrew D. Carson, Ph.D., with permission of the publisher. Copyright © 2004 by The Riverside Publishing Company. All rights reserved.

very high or very low, important insights or clinical hypotheses can be formed for individual cases, using the definitions in Table 6.2. Table 6.3 presents the names of the composites, the subtests included, the reliability of each composite, and the conversion equation necessary to transform the sums to the IQ metric ($M = 100$, $SD = 15$) for comparative purposes. All the composites in Table 6.3 have high reliability (.91 to .96), as calculated from the formula for composite reliability given in Tellegen and Briggs (1967). To calculate these composites, gather the SB5 subtest scaled scores and follow the example given in Rapid Reference 6.1.

Attention-Deficit/Hyperactivity Disorder

As many as 9% of boys and 3% of girls in North American schools show signs of Attention-Deficit/Hyperactivity Disorder (ADHD; Szatmari, 1992). The *Diagnostic and Statistical Manual of Mental Disorders–Fourth Edition* (*DSM-IV;* American Psychiatric Association, 2000) defines

Table 6.3 Shared-Ability Composites of SB5 Subtest Scaled Scores: Formula for Sums, Reliability, and Conversion Equations

Composite	Formula for Sum	Reliability	Equation
Planning Ability	NWM + VFR + VVS	.94	1.95(Sum) + 42.1
Trial-and-Error Problem Solving	NQR + NVS	.91	2.84(Sum) + 43.3
Visual-Motor Ability	NWM + NVS + VVS	.94	2.02(Sum) + 39.5
Abstract Conceptualization	VFR + VQR + VVS	.94	1.86(Sum) + 45.0
Understanding Long Questions	NQR + VQR + VVS	.94	1.86(Sum) + 44.7
Attention and Concentration	NFR + NWM + VVS + VWM	.95	1.56(Sum) + 37.8
Performance Under Time Pressure	NVS + NWM + VWM	.93	2.05(Sum) + 38.8
High Performers Under Time Pressure	NFR + NQR + NVS + NWM + VQR + VWM	.96	1.06(Sum) + 36.9
Cultural Knowledge	NKN + VFR + VKN	.94	1.93(Sum) + 42.7
Acquired Knowledge	NKN + VFR + VKN + VQR	.95	1.48(Sum) + 41.6
Intellectual Giftedness	NFR + NKN + NQR + VFR + VKN + VQR + VVS	.97	0.932(Sum) + 34.8

Source: The Intellectual Giftedness composite was developed by Roid (2003d) and others in Roid (2003a). Reproduced from the *Stanford-Binet Fifth Edition, Interpretive Manual* by Gale H. Roid, Ph.D, with permission of the publisher. Copyright © 2003 by The Riverside Publishing Company. All rights reserved.

Reproduced from the *Stanford-Binet Fifth Edition, Assessment Service Bulletin Number 4* by Gale H. Roid, Ph.D. and Andrew D. Carson, Ph.D, with permission of the publisher. Copyright © 2004 by The Riverside Publishing Company. All rights reserved.

Notes: Based on analysis of the SB5 normative sample (N = 4,800). Abbreviations are N for nonverbal, V for verbal, FR for Fluid Reasoning, QR for Quantitative Reasoning, VS for Visual-Spatial Processing, WM for Working Memory, and Sum for the sum of the scaled scores of the subtests in the composite.

subtypes of ADHD: the predominantly inattentive type, the hyperactive-impulsive type, and the combined type. Parents and teachers can easily describe the manifestations of the condition, including distractibility, poor listening skills, avoidance of tasks requiring sustained effort, fidgeting, inability to stay quietly seated, excessive talking, blurting out answers, and interrupting. Each of these behavior patterns forms part of the *DSM-IV* criteria for ADHD diagnosis. Volumes of research have been published on ADHD and it is impossible to summarize the findings and applications to assessment in this brief review. The reader should consult references such as those shown in Rapid Reference 6.3 to gain a thorough understanding of the disorder and its assessment.

≈ Rapid Reference 6.3

Bibliographic Notes on
Attention-Deficit/Hyperactivity Disorder (ADHD)

See the following references for more information, as noted, on ADHD:

- Criteria for ADHD are listed in *DSM-IV-TR* (American Psychiatric Association, 2000). This is the standard diagnostic tool for psychiatrists and psychologists, and it defines the three types of ADHD.

- Barkley (1990) is the definitive book by one of the world's recognized experts on ADHD.

- For a recent review of the assessment issues in ADHD, see Schwean and Saklofske (1998), which reviews applications to the Wechsler scales; or Taylor (2003), which reviews several instruments including Achenbachs' (2000), Connors (1997), and others.

- For a review of issues in adult ADHD, see Weiss, Murray, and Weiss (2002).

- The views of an American Medical Association council are discussed in Goldman, Genel, Bezman, and Slanetz (1998).

Roid (2003f) presents data on a sample of 94 students, aged 5 to 18, previously diagnosed with one of the three ADHD types by *DSM-IV* criteria. The sample was 74% male, as expected, and had a mixture of ethnicity and parental education levels. The pattern of SB5 mean scores for the sample showed a significantly lower Working Memory Factor Index score (90.2) in comparison to Fluid Reasoning (93.4), Quantitative Reasoning (95.9), Visual-Spatial Processing (95.1). The SB5 Knowledge Factor Index mean score (92.7) was not significantly different from that for Working Memory. This pattern of low memory scores combined with moderate crystallized (Knowledge) scores in an individual profile is similar to the classic "ACID" (Arithmetic, Coding, Information, Digit Span) pattern of the WISC-III subtest scores (Schwean & Saklofske, 1998). This pattern has typically been interpreted as showing the effects of distractibility on memory processing and delays in academic performance in ADHD cases.

Examiners using the SB5 with individuals who may have ADHD should be prepared for possible high levels of activity or inattentiveness of the examinee during testing. Having materials ready and out of reach of the child, sitting near the examinee (e.g., to retrieve materials), establishing rapport, gaining eye contact, using cues like "Ready?" and other techniques are strongly advised. The testing room should be free of distractions. Working with caregivers to prepare the child with extreme symptoms and using clear directions for rules of conduct (e.g., remain seated, focus on tasks) during testing may be necessary.

DON'T FORGET

Avoid the temptation to diagnose Attention-Deficit/Hyperactivity Disorder (ADHD) with only the scores obtained from cognitive tests. Thorough assessment of ADHD requires multiple sources of information in several settings, including ratings by teachers, parents, and peers, as well as medical information.

Assessment of Traumatic Brain Injury

Injury to the head that is serious enough to cause unconsciousness is one of the most serious pediatric disabilities among children in the United States (Ryan, Lamarche, Barth, & Boll, 1996). Traumatic brain injury (TBI) occurs more in males and is associated with car accidents, falls, recreational accidents, and child abuse, resulting in a complex of neuropsychological and cognitive difficulties (see Kamphaus, 2001, pp. 564–566, for more details). TBI cases can be difficult to test with any instrument if testing is attempted too soon after the injury, due to the disorientation and emotional trauma in the individual and the family. Examiners must be sensitive to these emotional difficulties and to the short attention span, fatigue, or other conditions that may be present in TBI cases—particularly among frail young children with communication difficulties. SB5 studies of TBI should begin to emerge in the literature as more of these difficult-to-access cases become available, as has been the case with WISC-III (Donders, 1997; Kamphaus, 2001).

In unpublished case studies submitted to the SB5 author, initial results show that TBI cases show profile weaknesses (low subtest scores relative to the individual's average for all 10 subtests) in Nonverbal Fluid Reasoning (NFR), Verbal Visual-Spatial Processing (VVS), the complex problems in Nonverbal Quantitative Reasoning (NQR), and both the Nonverbal and Verbal Working Memory subtests (NWM and VWM).[2] These weaknesses appear to be related to the well-documented effects of TBI on memory, mental-comparison processes (such as must occur in working memory tasks), visual-spatial processes, distractibility, and deficits in attention (Kamphaus, 2001; Lezak, 1995, p. 186). Use of the shared-ability composites on Attention-Concentration and Understanding Long Questions may be helpful in studying SB5 results for TBI

---

[2] The senior author thanks David Quinn, PsyD, of Ft. Meyers, Florida, for submitting the TBI cases.

cases (see Table 6.3). For example, a 52-year-old woman with traumatic head injuries had scaled scores of 9 (NFR), 11 (NKN), 6 (NQR), 8 (NVS), 6 (NWM), 14 (VFR), 8 (VKN), 7 (VQR), 4 (VVS), and 8 (VWM) (abbreviations are explained further in the note to Table 6.3). The 5-point difference between NFR and VFR was a statistically significant difference. Also, her low scores on NWM, NQR, and VVS were comparative weaknesses in her profile, compared to an average of 8.1 among all 10 subtest scores. Thus, the VVS subtest emerges as the most significant weakness in the profile, being significant in both statistical (.05 level) and infrequency (only 2% of population have VVS subtests lower than 4 points below the profile average) criteria. On the Attention-Concentration composite, this 52-year-old woman had a scaled-score total of 27, resulting in a composite score of 80, more than 1 standard deviation below the average of 100. On Understanding Long Questions, she had a sum of 17 (NQR = 6, VQR = 7, and VVS = 4), resulting in a very low composite of 76, nearly 2 standard deviations below average. In another adult TBI case, a 53-year-old man with a history of high educational attainment and creativity before the injury had subtest scores of 5 on NFR compared to 19 on VFR—a big difference! Also, he had low scores on NWM (6) and VWM (5) compared to a profile average of 10.6, again, highly significant weaknesses. Despite a score of 13 on VVS, this man had an Attention-Concentration composite of 92 compared to a Cultural Knowledge composite of 128 (NKN = 13, VKN = 12, and VFR = 19)—a huge 36-point difference!

Guidelines for Using the SB5 in Forensic Assessment

The SB5 can provide valuable information to professionals who may use intellectual assessments in courtroom or other legal proceedings as a component in forensic evaluations. The psychological evaluation report, which is prepared for use by the legal system, may carry significant weight in ultimate decisions arising from the courtroom. Psychological assessments are useful for assisting legal professionals, but the forensic evaluation does not answer ultimate legal questions. For example, *insanity* is a legal term and psychological assessments address the issue of insanity indirectly with exploration of awareness of surroundings, social judgment, interpersonal functioning, and intelligence. In a custody evaluation the assessments are utilized to inform the court of the psychological factors that bear upon the question of determining custodial arrangements. When a defendant asserts that he or she is not guilty by reason of insanity or diminished capacity, the evaluation provides information about the psychological functioning of that individual. It is important that the psychological report present facts to facilitate the legal process. Within this context of forensic evaluations, the SB5 may offer a wealth of useful information.

As a component in diagnosis or in assessing an individual's functional level, the SB5 provides meaningful information. Intellectual assessment may help a psychologist consider an individual's capacity to premeditate or create a plan of action, perhaps related to a crime. Very low levels of intelligence in adults may be indicative of diminished capacities, affecting the individual's ability to recognize the impact of her or his actions. Evaluating the mental state at the time of the offense often includes intellectual assessment. Such information will also assist with considering an individual's capacity to waive the Miranda warning and the subsequent admissibility of initial statements or confessions. Furthermore, intellectual functioning is a key component of considering competencies: competency to stand trial, to plead guilty, to testify, to participate, and ultimately, to be sentenced and possibly executed. Intelligence may be assessed to facilitate the consideration of what types of treatment or programming would be appropriate for an individual. An individual's IQ may also bear upon formulations regarding predictions of future offenses and relative dangerousness. Beyond this brief survey, there is a multitude of situations wherein intellectual assessment will be incorporated into the forensic evaluation, whether in criminal or civil courts. For additional information on forensic assessment, the reader should consult references such as Gregory (1996) or Hess and Weiner (1999).

Forensic evaluation reports should present testing data in clear and comprehensible formats to assist the legal proceedings. The rigor of the SB5's development and its broad clinical utility suggest that it will be an excellent instrument to include when assessing intellect. With anticipated research utilizing the SB5, the interpretive strength of results should increase progressively. As with other evaluations, the examiner should incorporate other assessment tools and address both consistent and possibly contradictory information. In both civil and criminal trial settings, the examinee may often have reason to behave in a negative light and produce scores that are below his or her actual intellectual capacities. Forensic evaluators must be mindful of these motivations and make efforts to evaluate malingering. Often, referrals for these evaluations will include requests to comment on the examinee's capacity to benefit from different forms of treatment. Understanding the performance variances within the SB5, an examiner can suggest whether an examinee has the capacity to understand and learn from treatment programs based upon behavioral, experiential, or cognitive modalities. Certainly, very low performance may indicate that an individual would have great difficulties benefiting from a treatment program that emphasizes written materials and abstract cognitive principles.

Assessment of the Gifted, "Twice-Exceptional" Individual

Specialists in the assessment of children and adults with exceptional intellectual giftedness provided important suggestions during the development of the SB5 (Roid, 2003c). Out of the 8 to 10 possible cognitive factors that could have been included in the SB5 (the total number in the full CHC model), experts in giftedness suggested an emphasis on reasoning abilities, resulting in the five factors that were ultimately chosen for the SB5. Also, speed of performance was deemphasized by reducing the number of timed subtests, because meticulous, gifted children are often punished by time bonuses. In addition, examiners are finding a growing group of "twice-exceptional" children (Kay, 2000) who are both intellectually gifted (e.g., FSIQ above 125 or 130) and diagnosed with ADHD, LD, or occasionally, autistic-like symptoms. The availability of the Working Memory subtests and the composites in Table 6.3 were designed to meet some of the assessment needs of the twice exceptional. One case study collected as part of the SB5 special-group studies (Roid, 2003f) was that of a 9-year-old boy with ADHD symptoms. He showed FSIQ of 130, and high scaled scores of 13 (NFR), 18 (NKN), 15 (NQR), 13 (NVS), 13 (NWM), 18 (VFR), 15 (VKN), 13 (VQR), 15 (VVS), and 13 (VWM). The lower scores on Working Memory subtests resulted in a Working Memory Factor Index of 117, a significant 13 points lower than his FSIQ. The Intellectual Giftedness composite in Table 6.3 was designed for such cases. Based on studies of gifted cases, the composite deletes the Working Memory subtests as well as the timed subtest NVS. The difficult Form Patterns tasks in NVS were found to be failed by some meticulous or twice-exceptional gifted children due to the time limits. In the profile of the 9-year-old boy, the Intellectual Giftedness composite is 135 and the Cultural Knowledge composite is 141, compared to 122 for the High Performers Under Time Pressure composite, giving support to the concern over timed tasks with gifted children.

In addition to the composites shown in Table 6.3, the new Extended IQ (EXIQ) scoring (see Chap. 3), available in the SB5 *Interpretive Manual* (Roid, 2003d), provides examiners with methods to evaluate the exceptionally and profoundly gifted. The EXIQ uses all the raw score points obtained by the examinee to calculate IQ values as high as 225. When individuals have both giftedness and LD, they may have exceptionally high scores in the verbal subtests such as Vocabulary (VKN), but low scores on Working Memory subtests. Because there is an implicit ceiling on the normalized scaled scores (all of the highest raw scores are truncated into a scaled score of 19), the conventional standard score IQ (e.g., FSIQ) may not show the full extent of the individual's giftedness. Use of the raw score–based EXIQ may allow additional range of measurement to be obtained.

Applications in Assessing Mental Retardation

Many questions were added to the lower levels of the SB5 to facilitate the assessment of children and adults with mental retardation. Blocks and other manipulatives were added to provide hands-on assessment tasks in this range of functioning. As with intellectual giftedness on the high end of the spectrum, individuals with extremely low functional levels may benefit from the new EXIQ (Roid, 2003d). The EXIQ ranges as low as 10 IQ, because sufficient raw score points are found at the very bottom of the subtest scales in unusual cases. Also, when subtests have raw scores of zero, only the EXIQ uses all the possible raw scores available in the test record. Occasionally, IQ scores in the 10 to 40 range are used for treatment planning or residential placement decisions among individuals with profound retardation.

🐾 TEST YOURSELF 🐾

1. What type of SB5 score is used to calculate shared-ability composites?

   (a) Scaled scores

   (b) Change-Sensitive Scores

   (c) Factor Index scores

   (d) IQ scores

   (continued)

2. **Which of the following did experts say was a primary limitation of the ability-achievement discrepancy method of identifying LD?**

   (a) Reliable test scores are lacking.

   (b) Two competing methods of discrepancy analysis are used.

   (c) The magnitude of differences between scores cannot be evaluated.

   (d) There are delays in identifying LD because reading achievement develops late in elementary school.

3. **Which of the following discrepancies between predicted and actual achievement scores in Reading Comprehension would be considered *greater* than the minimum discrepancy considered meaningfully significant and infrequent?**

   (a) 3 points

   (b) 8 points

   (c) 10 points

   (d) 20 points

4. **Which of the SB5 shared-ability composites is highest in reliability?**

   (a) Planning Ability

   (b) Abstract Conceptualization

   (c) Intellectual Giftedness

   (d) Cultural Knowledge

5. **Which four SB5 subtests were found to predict the early emergence of possible learning disabilities in reading?**

   (a) Nonverbal Fluid Reasoning

   (b) Nonverbal Knowledge

   (c) Nonverbal Quantitative Reasoning

   (d) Nonverbal Visual-Spatial Processing

   (e) Nonverbal Working Memory

   (f) Verbal Fluid Reasoning

   (g) Verbal Knowledge

   (h) Verbal Quantitative Reasoning

   (i) Verbal Visual-Spatial Processing

   (j) Verbal Working Memory

6. **What is the expected size of a meaningful discrepancy between IQ and achievement scores for slow learners?**

    (a) 8 points

    (b) 10 points

    (c) 15 points

    (d) 18 points

7. **Research on SB5 scores produced by young children with LD suggested that Working Memory is a good predictor of possible reading difficulties, along with which other SB5 factor?**

    (a) Fluid Reasoning

    (b) Knowledge

    (c) Quantitative Reasoning

    (d) Visual-Spatial Processing

8. **Shared-ability composites are combinations of subtest scaled scores converted to the IQ metric and used for clinical hypotheses.** True or False?

9. **The SB5 can be administered easily to examinees with traumatic brain injury on multiple occasions without fatigue or emotional reaction.** True or False?

10. **Forensic evaluations can utilize the SB5 to identify any of the following except**

    (a) cognitive limitations.

    (b) capacity to benefit from treatment.

    (c) insanity.

Answers: 1. a; 2. d; 3. d; 4. c; 5. b, e, g, j; 6. b; 7. b; 8. True; 9. False; 10. c

Seven

ILLUSTRATIVE CASE REPORTS

EVALUATION REPORT OF NORMAN C

Reason for Referral

Norman C. is a 14-year-old Caucasian male referred for intellectual functioning assessment by the director of a residential treatment center. His placement in this treatment center follows years of oppositional attitudes and defiance in the home. In the year prior to this evaluation, Norman was placed in psychiatric hospital units on multiple occasions for treatment of these issues and exhibited bizarre behaviors: paranoid ideation, extreme anxiety with new situations, and reports of visual and auditory hallucinations. While in formal treatment settings, Norman improved behaviorally with good compliance and significantly decreased psychotic symptoms. Despite the continuity of psychotropic medications across settings, Norman was consistently worse when in his home environment. A recent psychological evaluation confirmed diagnoses of Major Depressive Disorder, Schizoaffective Disorder–Depressive Type, Parent-Child Relational Problem, and Malingering. It was determined that Norman has exaggerated and fabricated psychotic symptoms to access treatment environments, which he prefers to his home. The clinical director hoped that the psychological evaluation could provide a better understanding of his cognitive issues pertinent to his ongoing treatment.

Background Information

Norman is the younger of two children in an intact family. His parents both work outside the home in professional careers. His parents described a healthy pregnancy, delivery, and early childhood with no history of major illness or injury. By age 3 years, Norman exhibited significant oppositional tendencies, which have continued through the present. Temper tantrums included yelling, striking out at his mother, and tearing apart his room. Emotional volatility was marked throughout his life, with frequent displays of immature playfulness. Norman often became very anxious when new toys arrived, or if his belongings were moved around. Norman had limited friendships and showed a preference for being alone. As an early adolescent, Norman reported suicidal ideation and a desire to kill several school peers. These risk factors led to the psychiatric hospitalizations.

Educational records indicated that Norman tested into an advanced placement program in the second grade. Over time his classroom performance declined, with poor organizational skills, difficulty completing work if alone or with peers, inattention, and emotional volatility. However, classroom observations in the previous academic year indicate that he has the capacity to attend and perform adequately.

Mental health treatment has included outpatient individual, family, and group counseling, psychiatric hospitalization, and the current residential treatment center. Current medications include an antidepressant and mood stabilizer. Family history of mental health difficulties is positive for maternal depression and paternal alcoholism.

Mental Status and Clinical Interview for Norman C

Norman presented as an alert, slender young man in good physical health. He was dressed casually with good hygiene. Norman spoke clearly and coherently. He demonstrated a tendency to explain his answers with multiple qualifying statements. Norman was fully oriented, except for some uncertainty regarding the current date. Eye contact was below normal limits. He sat comfortably without evidence of a psychomotor agitation or restlessness. He appeared to be easily distracted and at times made concerted yet polite efforts to change the task to a conversation topic he desired to engage. Norman presented a dysphoric mood and a broad range of affect. Norman was observed around his peers to be quiet and somewhat withdrawn. He showed considerable immature silliness during the evaluation. It appeared that Norman was attempting to engage in a different activity. Norman was able to describe the events of his treatment history in a manner consistent with records and collateral reports. However, it was notable that Norman failed to describe his experience of these events. He had a good sense for the facts, but little capacity to express his own experience in a meaningful manner. Historical and current suicidal and homicidal ideations were denied. During the clinical interview, Norman reported that auditory hallucinations continue, although with much less intensity and volume than last year. He refused to describe hallucinatory content to this evaluator, stating that he had been warned against such disclosures. This latter reference appeared to insinuate that the internal voice instructs him not to discuss the content. He acknowledged that he has exaggerated the experience of the hallucinations in an effort to be placed in treatment rather than live at home.

CAUTION

Avoid the temptation to provide more information than is requested. In some circumstances the test results could be explained in a single paragraph.

Test Results and Interpretation for Norman C.

Norman was administered the SB5 to assess his intellectual functioning. The SB5 includes 10 subtests, 5 within the nonverbal domain and 5 within the verbal domain. These two domains are assessed with subtests addressing multiple cognitive functions. The IQ and Factor Index scores of the battery have a mean of 100 and a standard deviation of 15, whereas the subtest scores range from 1 to 19 with a mean of 10 and standard deviation of 3. As shown in Table 7.1, Norman obtained a Full Scale IQ (FSIQ) score of 104, which classifies his intelligence in the average range and ranks him at the 61st percentile when compared with others his age. A 95% confidence interval suggests that his true score falls within the range of 100–108. The FSIQ provides a global summary of Norman's intellectual functioning and is a reliable measure of his general ability to reason, solve problems, and adapt to cognitive demands of the environment. He also obtained a

Table 7.1 Test Scores for Norman C.: Stanford-Binet Intelligence Scales–Fifth Edition (SB5)

	Nonverbal Subtests	Verbal Subtests	Factor Indexes (Percentiles)
Fluid Reasoning	11	11	106 (66)
Knowledge	12	12	111 (77)
Quantitative Reasoning	8	8	89 (23)
Visual-Spatial Processing	11	13	111 (77)
Working Memory	9	11	100 (50)
	IQ Scores	Percentiles	95% Confidence Interval
Nonverbal IQ	101	53	95–107
Verbal IQ	106	66	100–112
Full Scale IQ	104	61	100–108

Nonverbal IQ score of 101 and a Verbal IQ score of 106. The nonverbal domain of the SB5 requires less language ability and little or no vocal response. In contrast, the verbal domain requires expressive language or some degree of reading in certain items.

There was no statistically significant difference between the Nonverbal and Verbal IQ or subtest scores; thus it is reasonable to assume that his nonverbal and verbal skills are fairly evenly developed. Notable differences may sometimes be suggestive of language or visual-motor difficulties, learning problems, and the influence of psychoactive substances, among other possibilities. A more detailed interpretation of the Factor Index profile reveals that some variance occurred among the five different types of cognitive abilities measured by the indexes.

The Quantitative Reasoning (QR) Factor Index (89 points) was significantly below the other indexes except for Working Memory. The differences between QR and both Knowledge (KN) and Visual-Spatial Processing (VS) were 22 points each, a highly significant difference that occurs rarely in the general population. While his QR factor score was within a single standard deviation of the national average (100), the discrepancy from other indexes suggests some relative cognitive weak-

DON'T FORGET

Test Results and Interpretation

- Present scores in a format that will be understood by the readers of the report. Remember that some readers will not be familiar with statistical terms and implications. Include explanations for terms utilized and tailor the amount of detail to the intended audience for the report.

- If scores are presented in table form, be sure that the information is presented clearly and explained within the text of the report.

- Provide explanations of test components to help the reader understand the meaningfulness of various results.

nesses. In both verbal and nonverbal domains the subtests of this cognitive factor assess applied problem solving rather than specific mathematical knowledge acquired through school learning. Quantitative Reasoning requires concentration for long periods, attention to both verbal and visual cues, and patience during difficult tasks.

Working Memory (WM) assesses the capacity for Norman to store, transform, and retrieve information from short-term memory. These abilities are important in school and vocational environments for learning new tasks and incorporating new information. His scores were in the average range, suggesting a typical ability to maintain concentration and impulse control. The presence of internal stimuli, such as hallucinatory symptoms, in Norman would be expected to be markedly distracting. If he were distressed by such symptoms, it would be reasonable to assume that they would have an adverse effect on his capacity to manage these short-term memory tasks. The SB5 WM tasks require an examinee to attend to the stimulus presented by the examiner, recall it, manipulate the stimulus (in some cases), and then reproduce it for the examiner. It is a reasonable assumption that Norman's performance in this domain would have been lower than in other domains if psychotic symptoms were present. The slightly higher score in the verbal subtest of Working Memory may indicate some relative weakness in speed and precision of movement and tracking visual sequences as present in nonverbal WM. Norman's current medication regime should be considered as having a possible impact on his psychomotor speed and efficiency.

Norman's scores in Fluid Reasoning (FR) and KN subtests were the same in both nonverbal and verbal domains. Fluid Reasoning assesses the capacity to solve verbal and nonverbal problems with inductive or deductive reasoning. Norman demonstrated an average capacity to reason from specific information to the general rules and from general rules to the specific information, inferring appropriate conclusions from general examples. His score indicates adequate sequential reasoning, concentration, recognition of patterns, synthesis of information, and a tolerance for ambiguity. "Knowledge" assesses the accumulated general knowledge or information acquired from school, home, and other settings. This has often been referred to as a *crystallized ability* due to its reliance on learned material stored in long-term memory. Norman demonstrated high-average performance in recalling the meaning of words, a reflection of strong lexical knowledge and oral production. He also revealed strong skills in attention to visual detail and visual discrimination. Because KN is so much stronger in Norman than QR, his learned knowledge appears to be more in the reading or verbal arenas rather than the mathematical.

Visual-Spatial Processing (VS) measures the ability to recognize patterns, relationships, spatial orientations, and the Gestalt whole from a visual display of diverse pieces. Norman's scores reflected this capacity as a relative strength. The VS and KN subtests revealed the strongest performance. These results suggest a strength for Norman in VS, which may reflect a preferred visual style of learning.

Conclusions and Recommendations

Norman was provided with appropriate testing conditions for this assessment. He understood the instructions and appeared to give his best effort. The current medication regime may generate some slight reductions in psychomotor speed and efficiency, as observed in the nonverbal WM subtest. These SB5 scores and interpretations should provide an accurate representation of his current level of intellectual functioning. His overall intellectual level is classified as average and he is ranked at the 61st percentile. Norman appears to have the capacity to learn and retain a great deal of information; however, his capacity to reason and solve novel problems appears to be within the average range. Norman will likely find tasks that involve his facility with numbers and applied numerical problem solving to be more challenging. There are very few time limitations or scoring bonuses for quick performance within the

SB5. In academic settings with considerable time pressures, Norman may not produce work otherwise expected, given his performance on the SB5.

Norman demonstrates marked interpersonal deficits, cognitive distortions, and eccentricities of behavior that are consistent with features of Schizotypal Personality Disorder. The developmental history and clinical records are suggestive of a Schizoaffec-

> **DON'T FORGET**
>
> Referral questions can vary broadly. A clinical evaluation may ask for a broad amount of information regarding the psychological functioning of an examinee. The scope of the report should be guided by the referral questions. The report should be designed to help the intended audience understand the reasoning behind the conclusions.

tive Disorder–Depressive Type. His clinical symptom array is consistent with a partially remitted Major Depressive Disorder. His history is also consistent with Malingering, as he exaggerated his symptoms for external gain. The family interpersonal discord indicates the Parent-Child Relational Problem. Norman's immaturity and limited ability to cope with stressors generates distractibility and exaggerated activity levels. His cognitive rigidity may lead to poor coping with stressful situations, as evidenced by emotional volatility, displays of immaturity, and oppositional tendencies. Norman's average intellectual functioning level provides him with basic skills to establish necessary coping mechanisms. However, the family history suggests that Norman did not learn appropriate methods to manage stress. Thus, he matured with average intellectual skills, but without learning by instruction or modeling how to effectively manage frustrations. Norman has demonstrated good capacities to solve novel problems within the SB5; however, problems that are presented to him in the social world have greater time demands and continuous stimulus production. His impaired functioning is likely to have created sufficient personal frustration and self-doubt to generate emotional distress. His tendency to express himself in odd manners has created a self-reinforced cycle of negative attention-seeking.

Treatment needs to focus on addressing acute difficulties or problems and then the formation of goals related to preventing a recurrence of problems. Norman would benefit from learning to reduce his perceived anxiety so that he can feel comfortable slowing down his reaction times and thinking about situations prior to responding to them. In pursuit of such a goal, Norman will need to gain some confidence that his thinking can be an asset. Norman should be assisted to improve the clarity of his thinking and gradually implement flexibility in his beliefs. Therapy should address Norman's distorted beliefs, suspicious assumptions, and self-deprecating attitudes. Stress-inoculation training and other cognitive-behavioral interventions would be useful to help Norman learn to understand why he experiences difficulties interpersonally, and should provide opportunities for success. Group therapy and behavioral management programming should assist Norman with his difficulties both in interpersonal arenas and as they relate to his disruptive patterns of behavior. It would benefit him to frequently review interpersonal situations and conduct reality checks with trusted therapeutic professionals. As treatment progresses, the risk of suicidal ideation should continue to be assessed. Family-level interventions appear critical in this situation. The records suggest that the family would benefit from significant support to develop a comprehensive approach to reintegrating Norman into normalized relationships. Norman demonstrated some sense of entitlement to live in the setting in which he feels most comfortable. It may be that he has been reinforced to present himself in a negative light in an effort to obtain a particular type of structure and attention.

Norman is currently prescribed a significant amount of medication. It is important that Norman be medicated as needed, but not more than necessary. It is suggested that the treating medical professional review the recent psychological evaluation as well as this report and adjust the medication regime if appropriate. The tendency for Norman to exaggerate pathology to obtain desired outcomes should be noted.

This evaluation is based upon the current evaluation process and historical data. The accuracy of the information within this report may decline over time as Norman continues to mature and progress with treatment. Future users of this report's information should interpret the data with due consideration for the durability of results over time.

> ## CAUTION
>
> Minimize future misuse of the psychological report by indicating the limited validity of the report conclusions as time progresses. Psychological functioning may change over time and with life experiences, leading to variances on retests. Therapeutic experiences and educational programming may dramatically impact some evaluation results. Comments on the durability of the conclusions are useful at the beginning or the end of the report.

EVALUATION REPORT FOR JOSEPH K.

Reason for Referral

Joseph K. is a 28-year-old male evaluated at the request of his therapist from the county mental health treatment center. Joseph has recently initiated treatment within the county after his release from incarceration. His legal record includes a variety of misdemeanor theft and trespassing charges and two past convictions for driving while under the influence of alcohol. The most recent conviction results from charges that he made sexualized contact with a 15-year-old female cousin while intoxicated at a holiday party. In conjunction with his ongoing probation responsibilities, legal restitution, outpatient sex-offender treatment, and substance-addiction treatment, Joseph was referred for individual counseling. The therapist has requested this evaluation to better understand the client and obtain recommendations for treatment.

Background Information

Joseph's parents separated prior to his birth. Contact with his father occurred a few times during childhood and Joseph is currently unaware of his father's whereabouts. Joseph was removed from his mother's care when he was about 8 years old, following a child protective services investigation regarding parental neglect. Joseph then recalls moving around to several different foster homes until he was 18. Joseph denied any experience of physical or sexual abuse. There is no history of significant illnesses or injuries. He retained contact with his mother and reported that they now have a good relationship. Joseph graduated from high school and recalls that school was often boring and difficult. Employment consisted of several brief odd jobs until he secured a position at a local manufacturing plant, where he was employed for 5 years until his arrest. Living in the same town throughout his life, Joseph maintained friendships from his school years. Joseph does not have a history of long-lasting romantic relationships. In his description, he reported that few relationships lasted more than 4 months. He acknowledged that he has engaged in petty theft activities and consumed alcohol excessively since about age 18. Joseph denied any illegal substance abuse, except for a few episodes of smoking marijuana.

Five years ago, Joseph was found guilty of sexual contact with a minor. According to the records, Joseph fondled a 15-year-old female cousin while at a holiday gathering. He reported that he was heavily intoxicated at the time of the incident. Joseph served time in prison and has recently been released on parole. During his incarceration, Joseph participated in a drug- and alcohol-abuse program. He is now participating in mandated substance-abuse treatment as well as sex-offender treatment. Both of these interventions occur in a group format. The therapists for these interventions referred Joseph for individual counseling to address depressive symptoms.

Mental Status and Clinical Interview for Joseph K.

Joseph presented for the evaluation as a physically healthy individual. He was dressed in clean clothes with good hygiene. He sat stiffly during the evaluation activities with some apparent nervousness regarding the evaluation process. Joseph was fully oriented, expressing a clear understanding of the evaluation purpose, and of identity, location, and date. He spoke clearly and coherently with some tendency to low volume. He was polite and attentive and maintained fair concentration throughout our appointment. Joseph demonstrated a dysphoric mood and constricted range of affect. Hallucinatory experiences were denied. Joseph denied any historical or current suicidal or homicidal ideation.

Test Results and Interpretation for Joseph K.

To address the referral questions, the SB5 and the Millon Clinical Multiaxial Inventory–Third Edition (MCMI-III) were administered (Millon, 1994). These instruments were selected to provide meaningful additive information to the clinical picture of Joseph.

The MCMI-III is a personal-

> ### DON'T FORGET
>
> - Discuss the strengths and weaknesses of an individual. Avoid a biased reporting style that addresses either strengths or weaknesses in isolation.
> - Explain contradictory information within the test results.
> - Avoid writing in casual or elaborate language. The most useful reports will provide evaluation information in a straightforward manner.

ity inventory that compares an individual's responses against a national sample. The validity scales indicated that Joseph's responses demonstrated some mild self-deprecating tendencies. This response style was not sufficient to invalidate the clinical scale information. The clinical scales revealed that Joseph has marked similarities with depressive and pessimistic individuals. He is likely to often feel cheated and unappreciated by others. Other men with similar response patterns are often conflicted between desires to be nurtured and angry self-assertion. Joseph appears to approach others with a pattern of self-pitying negativism, punctuated by periodic angry outbursts. Such tension is likely to contribute to impulsive behavior tendencies. His expectation of negative outcomes likely leads him to act in a negative or irritable manner, which increases the likelihood that his expectations will be fulfilled. This pattern may lend to difficulty in maintaining close relationships over time.

The SB5 administration revealed information about his intellectual functioning. (Scores from this administration are presented below.) During the administration, Joseph was cooperative and followed instructions well. Standardized administration procedures were followed, so it can be assumed that the results will provide reliable information regarding his intellectual functioning. As shown in Table 7.2, Joseph's performance resulted in a Full Scale IQ (FSIQ) score of 93, Nonverbal IQ (NVIQ) score of 97, and Verbal IQ (VIQ) score of 90. The two cognitive domains of nonverbal (seeing visual trends) and verbal (comprehending words and spoken directions) are assessed with subtests addressing multiple cognitive functions. The nonverbal sections of the SB5 require less language ability or little to no vocal response, while the verbal sections require some expressive language or degree of reading in difficult items. The difference between the nonverbal and verbal domains was slight except for one of the cognitive functions (Working Memory). It is likely that Joseph's vocational and recreational activities exercised his nonverbal capacities while promoting less use of more

Table 7.2 Test Scores for Joseph K.: Stanford-Binet Intelligence Scales–Fifth Edition (SB5)

	Nonverbal Subtests	Verbal Subtests	Factor Indexes (Percentiles)
Fluid Reasoning	12	11	109 (73)
Knowledge	11	12	108 (70)
Quantitative Reasoning	7	8	86 (18)
Visual-Spatial Processing	8	6	82 (12)
Working Memory	10	5	86 (18)
	IQ Scores	Percentiles	95% Confidence Interval
Nonverbal IQ	97	42	91–103
Verbal IQ	90	25	84–96
Full Scale IQ	93	32	89–97

verbal skills. The lack of a significant difference between the NVIQ and VIQ scores suggests that the FSIQ score provides a global summary of Joseph's intellectual functioning and is a reliable measure of his general ability to reason, solve problems, and adapt to cognitive demands of the environment. Joseph's FSIQ is at the 32nd percentile in a national sample. A 95% confidence interval suggests that his true FSIQ score falls within the range of 89 to 97.

The Factor Indexes and IQ scores have a mean of 100 and a standard deviation of 15. The Factor Indexes produced by Joseph during this SB5 administration reveal some marked performance discrepancies. The Fluid Reasoning (FR) index score was within the average range, but at the 73rd percentile. This index assesses the ability to utilize inductive and deductive reasoning. This suggests that Joseph has a strong ability to reason from the part to the whole or to identify implications or conclusions from reviewing general information. Joseph's performance did not reveal significant differences between the nonverbal and verbal domains. Joseph obtained a score at the 70th percentile in the Knowledge (KN) index. As with the FR index, Joseph demonstrated very similar capacities across nonverbal and verbal domains in the KN index, which assesses the accumulated fund of information acquired throughout life. It demands that such information be accurately retrieved from storage in long-term memory. The final three indexes were notably lower than FR and KN: Quantitative Reasoning (QR) assessed Joseph's abilities with numerical problem solving at the 18th percentile. No significant differences occurred between the Nonverbal and Verbal QR domains with applied problem-solving items. Visual-Spatial Processing (VS) assessed Joseph's ability to recognize patterns and relationships at the 12th percentile. Again, no notable difference occurred across the two domains. The Working Memory (WM) index assessed Joseph's capacity to store information in short-term memory and transform it, and the index was low—at the 18th percentile.

The SB5 includes 10 subtests, 5 within the nonverbal domain and 5 within the verbal domain. The subtest scores range from 1 to 19 with a mean of 10 and standard deviation of 3. The WM scores revealed a significant difference between the nonverbal and verbal subtests (10 vs. 5) and the difference of 5 points occurs rarely in the general population. Joseph obtained an average-range score in the nonverbal domain, suggesting that he has adequate capacities to store, manipulate, and retrieve visual information in short-term memory. In contrast, a relative weakness appeared with the verbal WM. Joseph had much greater difficulty with retaining and manipulating information presented verbally.

Conclusions and Recommendations

Joseph presents with a history consistent with alcoholism and symptoms of a mood disorder. The MCMI indicated that he has depressive traits. Individuals with depressive traits often exhibit impaired performance with tasks that involve sustained concentration and cognitive manipulation of information. It is likely that Joseph experiences a major mood disorder, such as Dysthymic Disorder or Major Depressive Disorder–Chronic. The treatment provider may wish to assess for historical depressive episodes to identify the most accurate diagnosis. Joseph has a history of illegal behavior; however, other indicators do not confirm a diagnosis of Antisocial Personality Disorder. Joseph's long history of alcoholism is an important issue for treatment, although the SB5 assessment does not suggest global memory impairments.

> **DON'T FORGET**
>
> Answer the referral questions. The referral questions may suggest very narrow interpretations and limited conclusion statements, as in situations where the evaluation has been requested to determine IQ scores. A forensic evaluation may be requested to assess an examinee's capacity to waive Miranda rights, or his or her potential responsiveness to treatment programming.

The SB5 results suggest that Joseph has average global intelligence. He will be able to think through basic problems presented visually and verbally. The referral information indicates that Joseph is involved in three therapeutic treatment activities at the same time. Joseph may become confused or apathetic if the treatment providers unknowingly present him with contradictory information or suggestions. With his history, it is important to avoid this dilemma when possible to reduce his risks for engaging in risk-taking behaviors. Joseph does not have the personality style to advocate for himself and productively negotiate conflicts between his treatment professionals. It will be helpful for Joseph to be provided with concrete courses of action for managing the multiple treatment activities.

It is important to note that Joseph will have some difficulties with recalling significant amounts of verbal information and utilizing it in a meaningful manner. In treatment settings, it may be particularly useful to present concepts and tasks in both verbal and visual formats. Joseph will likely retain information in a more useful manner when it is presented in multiple modalities—through discussion, experiential exercise, and written materials. Reviewing the content of previous therapy sessions will also improve likely treatment results over time. Joseph's depressive moods and negativistic personality style may exacerbate a failure mentality. The therapeutic adaptations presented here could provide Joseph with some experience of success. For example, the review of sessions could both improve his retention and be a source of recognizing his progress toward therapy goals.

Individual psychotherapy should be designed to address Joseph's depressed moods. A referral for a psychiatric consultation would be appropriate. Joseph exhibited multiple self-defeating behavior and thought patterns. He also has experienced multiple interpersonal losses from his childhood and adulthood that contribute to his present emotional functioning and personality style. Helpful treatment modalities may include cognitive-behavioral, solution-focused, and interpersonal techniques. Joseph has the intellectual capacities to reason how common themes may be prevalent over multiple situations. With limited explanation, Joseph should be able to understand therapeutic concepts. His intellectual testing results suggest a heightened need for the therapist to check his comprehension and retention of necessary information. Individual therapy sessions may also provide a productive opportunity to review experiences in other treatment settings.

This evaluation is based upon the current evaluation process and historical data. The accuracy of the information within this report may decline over time. Future users of this report's information should interpret the data with due consideration for the durability of results over time.

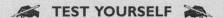

TEST YOURSELF

1. It is important to address a wide variety of information within the report and comment on issues not specifically addressed by the referral questions. True or False?

2. In the referral section of the report, be sure to include all of the following except

   (a) information about the referral source.

   (b) specific referral questions or issues.

   (c) a summary of current issues related to the request for the evaluation.

   (d) responses to the referral questions.

3. In the Test Results and Interpretation section of the report, what information is not appropriate?

   (a) Explanation of test scores

   (b) Straightforward information about the examinee's performance

   (c) Intriguing and unexplained contradictory information

   (d) Concise descriptions of subtests

4. Interpretation of the SB5 results should be presented in more than a single paragraph. True or False?

5. The examinee's physical appearance and emotional condition should never be discussed in the background information. True or False?

6. Which of the following is not a good suggestion for the Test Results and Interpretation section of a clinical report?

   (a) Discuss both strengths and weaknesses.

   (b) Include as many statistics as possible.

   (c) Clearly explain the meaning of test scores.

   (d) Explain any apparent contradictions in the results.

7. The SB5 test administration procedures used for Norman C. and Joseph K. are good examples of the use of accommodations and test modifications. True or False?

(continued)

8. **Which of Joseph K.'s subtest scaled scores showed the greatest nonverbal versus verbal differences?**

   (a) Knowledge

   (b) Quantitative Reasoning

   (c) Visual-Spatial Processing

   (d) Working Memory

9. **Both case studies presented in this chapter showed Full Scale IQ in the average range (90 to 109).** True or False.

Answers: 1. False; 2. d; 3. c; 4. False; 5. False; 6. b; 7. False; 8. d; 9. True

Appendix A

SB5 Interpretive Worksheet: Seven-Step Interpretive Method[1]

Step 1: Assumptions

Answer the following questions to determine whether you can use the published norms to interpret SB5 scores with confidence. If you answer any of the following questions in the affirmative, you should correct the deficiency, use alternative scoring (such as using the Nonverbal IQ only, using change-sensitive scores, or using age equivalents—see Step 7). If you feel the test session was invalid, you may have to retest the examinee after a suitable waiting period (e.g., 6 months).

(a) Were standard administration procedures adapted or changed in a significant way?

(b) Were any errors made in tabulating raw scores or converting raw scores to standard scores?

(c) Did you discover that accommodations were needed during testing (e.g., sign language for individuals with deafness or a special response keyboard for an individual with severe motor disabilities), and do you feel the test session did not produce a valid measurement of the examinee?

Step 2: Background and Context of the Examinee

You should make every effort to check the background of the examinee and the context in which he or she lives, including the language spoken

---

[1] The seven-step interpretive strategy is reproduced from the *Stanford-Binet Fifth Edition, Interpretive Manual* by Gale H. Roid, Ph.D., with permission of the publisher. Copyright © 2003 by The Riverside Publishing Company. All rights reserved.

at home, work, or school. Also, check to see if the examinee is being treated (or has ever been treated) for vision or hearing difficulties, speech and language disabilities, or communication disorders. Because the SB5 requires a degree of English language competence (understanding of brief oral instructions in English at a minimum), the relative language ability and English language dominance of the examinee are of vital concern. Try to establish through interviews with the examinee, parents, caregivers, peers, teachers, and so on, or from the cumulative record of the individual (if available), the degree of usage and mastery of English versus an alternative language. If the examinee is receiving training in or is enrolled in an official school program such as English Language Learner (ELL), English as a Second Language (ESL), or Limited English Proficiency (LEP), you can infer that the examinee will have some difficulty with SB5 instructions or items, particularly in the verbal sections of the test. Additionally, in interviews with the examinee or others, ask some of the following questions.

(a) Degree of English language dominance and acculturation
- Does the examinee speak a language other than English?
- Was the examinee raised in a country other than the host country?
- Does the examinee report the use of non-English language(s) in the home or elsewhere?
- Is there any sign of non-English language usage during the test session?
- Did the parents, guardians, or other persons accompanying the examinee speak non-English languages before, during, or after the testing session?

If any of the above are answered in the affirmative, ask some of the following questions:
   1. Which language is used most frequently at home, work, or school?

2. Does the examinee and/or his or her parents/
   guardians do any of the following?
   - Live near or socialize principally with individuals
     who regularly speak the non-English language(s)
   - Prefer reading material or visual and audio media
     presented in the non-English language(s)
   - Report a strong preference for maintaining the cul-
     ture and language of their country of origin instead
     of English (Western or American) culture and lan-
     guage

(b) Possible difficulties or disabilities that may require accom-
    modations or adaptations of the SB5
    - Do records show or the examinee (or parents/guardians)
      report that any of the following are present or have been
      present in the past?
    1. Color blindness
    2. Poor visual acuity (uncorrected) or blindness
    3. Hard-of-hearing or deafness conditions
    4. Severe motor (orthopedic) difficulties, delays, or dis-
       abilities
    5. Severe speech, articulation, language, or communica-
       tion difficulties or disabilities
    6. Recent or current illness or medical treatment, includ-
       ing current use of prescription medicine
    7. Any other prior or current difficulty, disability, or de-
       velopmental delay that could require significant accom-
       modation or adaptation of the test administration
       methods

If any evidence exists to show that the examinee may have or did have
language-dominance, acculturation, difficulty, delay, or disability issues,
weigh the evidence, report it in any summary report of SB5 testing, and

consider the degree to which it may affect the interpretation of SB5 scores. If significant accommodations or adaptations of SB5 standard test administration methods were used (or were needed but unused), consider using qualitative or alternative scoring and interpretive methods rather than normative standard scores (see Step 7).

Step 3: Examine Nonverbal IQ and Verbal IQ and Evaluate Any Difference That May Occur

Complete the following table and evaluate the size of any difference between NVIQ and VIQ before proceeding to the next step. The difference must have both statistical significance and infrequency in the normative population (occurring in 15% of the population or less) to be considered important.

NVIQ Value	VIQ Value	Difference (Diff)	Significance of the Difference at the .05 Level	Frequency (%) in the Normative Population	Comparison and Conclusion
			Ages 2–9 Diff > 9	Diff > 13 (15%)	Is the difference 14 points or greater?
			Ages 10–13 Diff > 10	Diff > 18 (5%)	
			Ages 14+ Diff > 8		

Step 4: Interpret the SB5 Full Scale IQ

Complete the following chart, using the description in Table A.1. Take caution in interpreting and using FSIQ if there was an important difference between Nonverbal IQ and Verbal IQ (see Step 3).

Sum of Scaled Scores	Full Scale IQ	Confidence Interval 90% or 95% (circle one)	Percentile Rank	Descriptive Category from Table A.1

Table A.1 Descriptive Categories for Various Levels of SB5 Full Scale IQ Including Extended IQ Score Ranges

IQ Range	Extended Category Description	Description for General Use
176–225	Profoundly gifted or profoundly advanced	Profoundly advanced
161–175	Extremely gifted or extremely advanced	Extremely advanced
145–160	Very gifted or highly advanced	Highly advanced
130–144	Gifted or very advanced	Very advanced
120–129	Superior	Superior
110–119	High average	High average
90–109	Average	Average
80–89	Low average	Low average
70–79	Borderline impaired or delayed	Borderline delayed
55–69	Mildly impaired or delayed	Mildly delayed
40–54	Moderately impaired or delayed	Moderately delayed
25–39	Severely impaired or delayed	Severely delayed
10–24	Profoundly impaired or delayed	Profoundly delayed

Source: Adapted from Roid, 2003d. Reproduced from the *Stanford-Binet Fifth Edition, Interpretive Manual* by Gale H. Roid, Ph.D., with permission of the publisher. Copyright © 2003 by The Riverside Publishing Company. All rights reserved.

Step 5: Interpretation of Differences Among the Factor Index Scores

Complete the following table and evaluate the size of any difference between the pairs of factor index scores listed below. The difference must have both statistical significance and infrequency in the normative population (occurring in 15% of the population or less) to be considered important.

First Factor Index	Second Factor Index	Difference	Size of Difference That Is Both Statistically Significant and Infrequent		Important difference? (yes or no)
			15% level	5% level	
FR	KN		19	27	
FR	QR		19	26	
FR	VS		19	27	
FR	WM		19	27	
KN	QR		18	26	
KN	VS		18	25	
KN	WM		19	26	
QR	VS		17	24	
QR	WM		18	25	
VS	WM		18	25	

Source: Roid (2003f). Adapted and reproduced from the *Stanford-Binet Fifth Edition, Technical Manual* by Gale H. Roid, Ph.D., with permission of the publisher. Copyright © 2003 by The Riverside Publishing Company. All rights reserved.

Note. FR = Fluid Reasoning, KN = Knowledge, QR = Quantitative Reasoning, VS = Visual-Spatial Processing, and WM = Working Memory.

Step 6: Interpret Differences Among the SB5 Subtest Scaled Scores That Suggest Strengths and Weaknesses in Cognitive Function

Complete the following tables and evaluate the size of any difference between each SB5 subtest scaled score and the average of all 10 subtests in the examinee's profile. First, calculate the average score across all 10 subtests, then compare each subtest score to the average. The significantly higher subtest scores suggest cognitive strengths, and the significantly lower subtest scores suggest relative cognitive weaknesses in the individual. To be considered important and indicative of a strength or weakness, the difference must have both statistical significance and infrequency in the normative population (occurring in 5% of the population or less, as a conservative guideline).

Enter Nonverbal Scores Here					Enter Verbal Scores Here					Calculate Average (get sum and divide by 10)
FR	KN	QR	VS	WM	FR	KN	QR	VS	WM	

Source: Roid (2003f).

Note. FR = Fluid Reasoning, KN = Knowledge, QR = Quantitative Reasoning, VS = Visual-Spatial Processing, and WM = Working Memory.

Domain and Subtest Name	Enter Scaled Score	Enter Average Score	Difference Value Significant at .05 Level and Infrequent (5% or less) in Normative Population	Is this a strength or weakness? (high/low)
Nonverbal Subtests				
Fluid Reasoning			5	
Knowledge			4	
Quantitative Reasoning			4	
Visual-Spatial Processing			4	
Working Memory			4	
Verbal Subtests				
Fluid Reasoning			4	
Knowledge			4	
Quantitative Reasoning			4	
Visual-Spatial Processing			4	
Working Memory			4	

Source: Roid (2003f). Adapted and reproduced from the *Stanford-Binet Fifth Edition, Technical Manual* by Gale H. Roid, Ph.D., with permission of the publisher. Copyright © 2003 by The Riverside Publishing Company. All rights reserved.

Step 7: Use of Optional Scoring and Qualitative Interpretation

1. To interpret the factor index scores for parents, teachers, or others, you may want to convert the raw-score totals for each

factor into change sensitive scores (CSS; see page 2 of the SB5 record form) and then into age equivalents.

2. To document possible growth or change due to treatment, instruction, or other interventions, record the present CSS scores for the examinee and retest her or him in 6- to 12-month increments (e.g., at the beginning and end of each academic year). The CSS scores will be more sensitive to change than the normative standard scores in most cases.

3. Study the chart in Appendix C. After standard SB5 testing is complete, test the examinee's limits by allowing more time, repeating items, or other methods described in Appendix C.

Appendix B

Tables of Definitions and Descriptions of Cognitive Abilities and Components of SB5 Factor Index and Subtest Scores

Table B.1 Definitions of the CHC Theory Cognitive Components (Stratum I Abilities) Hypothesized as Elements of the SB5 Factor Index Scores

Stratum I Ability (Code)	Definition
Induction (I)	To inspect a set of materials (verbal or nonverbal) and identify the common characteristic, rule, concept, process, or trend underlying the material
General Sequential Reasoning (RG)	To solve a verbal or nonverbal problem by starting with stated premises, rules, or conditions and reaching a logical conclusion based on the information provided
Lexical Knowledge (VL)	To understand the meanings of words, as in vocabulary tests, as part of one's general fund of verbal knowledge
General Information (KO)	To be able to access and use one's fund of general knowledge, acquired by storing information at home, school, work, and so on
Oral Production & Fluency (OP)	To show fluency and clarity in producing a story or description (e.g., of a picture); amount of talkativeness
Quantitative Reasoning (RQ)	To understand quantitative concepts and procedures and apply them in solving verbal or nonverbal problems with induction or deduction
Mathematical Knowledge (KM)	To demonstrate general knowledge of mathematical concepts and methods

Table B.1 Continued

Stratum I Ability (Code)	Definition
Visualization (VZ)	To perceive visual patterns, manipulate them in one's "mind's eye," and predict how they would look when altered
Spatial Relations (SR)	To rapidly manipulate visual objects and visual patterns to "see" them from different angles or perspectives (e.g., mental rotation, visual transformation)
Closure Speed (CS)	To quickly apprehend and identify a visual pattern, without knowing in advance what the pattern is, when the pattern is disguised or obscured in some way
Memory Span (MS)	To accurately recall an increasingly long series of verbal, numerical, or figural material, in correct order, after one exposure to the material
Visual Memory (MV)	To visually scan and store visual material presented once and then recall the material in correct order during a recall phase of a task (especially where the material cannot be verbally encoded easily)
Serial Perceptual Integration (PI)	To perceive and identify a visual pattern presented serially or successively, part by part, at a rapid rate
Language Development (LD)	To demonstrate general development of spoken native language skills, but not specifically reading ability

Source: Adapted from Roid, 2003d. Reproduced from the *Stanford-Binet Fifth Edition, Interpretive Manual* by Gale H. Roid, Ph.D., with permission of the publisher. Copyright © 2003 by The Riverside Publishing Company. All rights reserved.

Table B.2 Activities Found in the SB5 Testlets Hypothesized to Measure Cognitive Components (Stratum I Abilities) within the Five SB5 Factor Indexes

Cognitive Component	Fluid Reasoning (FR)	Knowledge (KN)	Quantitative Reasoning (QR)	Visual-Spatial Processing (VS)	Working Memory (WM)
Induction (I)	Matrices, verbal absurdities				
General Sequential Reasoning (RG)	Object-series, early reasoning, analogies				
Lexical Knowledge (VL)		Vocabulary			
General Information (KO)		Procedural knowledge, picture absurdities			
Oral Production & Fluency (OP)	Early reasoning	Procedural knowledge, picture absurdities			
Quantitative Reasoning (RQ)			All activities		

Mathematical Knowledge (KM)			All activities		
Visualization (VZ)				Form board, form patterns	
Spatial Relations (SR)				Position and direction	
Closure Speed (CS)				Form patterns	
Memory Span (MS)					All activities
Visual Memory (MV)	Early reasoning, matrices				Block span
Serial Perceptual Integration (PI)					Block span
Language Development (LD)		Vocabulary			Memory for sentences, last word

Table B.3 Descriptions of the Content and Cognitive Abilities Measured by the Ten SB5 Subtests

Content or Ability	Description
Nonverbal Fluid Reasoning: Object-Series/Matrices	Measures the ability to solve novel problems presented in visual form without reliance on academic or culturally bound information. Abilities include inductive and deductive reasoning to identify visual sequences and analogical patterns. For young children and lower-functioning examinees, the subtest measures the ability to identify shapes, such as circles and triangles, and to use color, size, and shape concepts to identify sequences and patterns. For older and advanced examinees, the subtest measures inductive reasoning of matrix analogy problems, using symbolic and visual content.
Verbal Fluid Reasoning	Measures the ability to solve novel verbal problems and to vocalize correct explanations of solutions to these problems. For young children and lower-functioning individuals, the subtest measures the ability to identify cause and effect relationships depicted in illustrations; classify pictorial objects by similarity of form and function; and explain answers. For older and advanced individuals, the subtest measures inductive reasoning with verbally absurd statements and verbal analogies.
Nonverbal Knowledge	Measures the acquisition of general information and the oral production of explanations of absurdities occurring in nature, among people, and in social situations. For young children and lower-functioning individuals, the subtest measures verbal comprehension of gestures and nonverbal signals based on graded word lists of common objects and activities. For older and advanced individuals, the subtest measures the crystallized ability to identify missing parts or absurd features of illustrations. Also, advanced examinees must use their fund of general information and language development to explain the location and nature of the missing part or the absurdity.

Table B.3 Continued

Content or Ability	Description
Verbal Knowledge: Vocabulary	Measures lexical knowledge and language development in terms of the breadth of vocabulary acquisition and mastery. Vocabulary is a strong predictor of general ability, school achievement, and vocational advancement, given the reliance of these settings on the verbal knowledge and verbal comprehension measured by the subtest. For young children and lower-functioning individuals, the subtest measures the understanding of common terms used to describe one's body; pictures of common objects; and typical actions of people. For older and advanced individuals, the subtest measures the comprehension of increasingly difficult and unusual English words.
Nonverbal Quantitative Reasoning	Measures the ability to apply logical thinking and mathematical knowledge to the solution of pictorially presented quantitative problems. For young children and lower-functioning individuals, the subtest measures basic recognition of numbers, addition, and estimation. For older and advanced individuals, the subtest measures the identification of figural and numerical series and the use of linear transformations, algebraic principles, and systems of equations to solve quantitative problems presented in illustrations.
Verbal Quantitative Reasoning	Measures mathematical conceptualization, identification of mathematical relationships, and logical reasoning in the solution of verbally presented quantitative problems. For young children and lower-functioning individuals, the subtest measures fundamental quantitative concepts and processes such as numbering and counting, addition, and subtraction. For older and advanced individuals, the subtest measures mathematical reasoning and word problems with multiplication and advanced logical and mathematical analysis.

(continued)

Table B.3 Continued

Content or Ability	Description
Nonverbal Visual-Spatial Processing	Measures various components of visualization, spatial reasoning, and the ability to complete a visual form by assembling its parts. For young children and lower-functioning individuals, the subtest uses the classic form board to assess visualization of common shapes, one-to-one correspondence, and spatial perceptions. For older and advanced individuals, the subtest measures spatial relations and closure speed in assembling puzzle-like forms from an extended set of form board pieces, assessing the ability to construct the whole from its parts.
Verbal Visual-Spatial Processing	Measures various components of visualization and spatial reasoning, requiring verbal explanation of spatial relationships depicted in illustrations and verbal descriptions. For young children and lower-functioning individuals, the subtest assesses the understanding of verbal spatial concepts such as "inside," or "behind," requiring receptive language skills in responding to maps and illustrations. For older and advanced individuals, the subtest measures verbal skills in describing the path to follow on maps and illustrations, and comprehension of verbal descriptions of spatial orientations ("Go east, turn right . . .").
Nonverbal Working Memory	Measures the ability to store, transform, and retrieve visual information in short-term memory. For young children and lower-functioning individuals, the subtest measures short-term memory and attention, such as in locating a hidden toy, and, later, the recall of sequences of block taps. For older and advanced individuals, the subtest measures working memory—the ability to transform sequences of block taps by mentally sorting them into two categories.

Table B.3 Continued

Content or Ability	Description
Verbal Working Memory	Measures the ability to store, transform, and retrieve verbal information in short-term memory. For young children and lower-functioning individuals, the subtest measures short-term memory of sentences—the ability to repeat vocally a stated sentence. For older and advanced individuals, the subtest emphasizes working memory—the ability to transform a series of questions by sorting out the last word in each sentence—an important cognitive ability in holding and sorting through verbal information.

Table B.4 Cognitive Abilities Hypothesized as Processes Underlying Performance on the SB5 Subtests

	Nonverbal					Verbal				
	FR	KN	QR	VS	WM	FR	KN	QR	VS	WM
Information Processing										
Visualization of Abstract Stimuli	P									
Visualization of Meaningful Stimuli	S	P		P		S			S	
Inspection of Objects by Touch	S			P						
Attention to Verbal Cues	P	S	S			P	S	S	P	S
Attention to Visual Cues	P	S	S	S	S					
Impulse Control				S	P					P
Concentration for Long Periods	P		P	S	S	S		P	S	S
Freedom from Distractibility		S			P	S				P
Freedom from Visual Neglect	S	P		P	S				S	
Toleration of Ambiguity	S	P				S				
Patience with Difficult Tasks	S		S	S	P			S	S	P
Speed of Movement				S	P					

Process						
Precision of Movement	P	S	S	P		
Systematic Visual Scanning	P	S	S	S	S	
Wide Auditory Attention Span	S	S	S	S	P	
Problem Solving						
Search Strategies	P	P	S	S	P	S
Mental Review of Potential Answers	P	S	P	S		
Relating Verbal Parts to Whole	P	P	S	S	S	
Visual Discrimination	P	S	S	S		
Tracking Visual Sequences	P	S	P			
Pattern Recognition	P	S				
Mental Verbal Mediation	P	S	S			
Fund of General Information	S	S	P			
Knowledge of Culturally Relevant Facts	S	S				
Abstract Verbal Concepts	S	S	S			
Verbal Fluency	P	P	S	S		
Rapid Retrieval of Words and Explanations	P	P	S	S		
Planning Ability	P	S	S	S		

(continued)

Table B.4 Continued

	Nonverbal					Verbal				
	FR	KN	QR	VS	WM	FR	KN	QR	VS	WM
Trial-and-Error Strategies	S	S	S	P		S		S		
Synthesis of Information	P	S	S			S	S	S		
Reproduction of Models				P						
Cognitive Flexibility	S	S	S	S		S		S		
Retention Span					P					P
Visualization of Whole from Parts				P					S	
Recognition and Evaluation of Parts	S	S	S	P		S		S	P	
Production of Conventional Answers		S	P				S	P		
Production of Creative Answers				P		P		S	S	

Source: Adapted from Roid, 2003d. Reproduced from the *Stanford-Binet Fifth Edition, Interpretive Manual* by Gale H. Roid, Ph.D., with permission of the publisher. Copyright © 2003 by The Riverside Publishing Company. All rights reserved.

Note. Abbreviations are as follows: FR = Fluid Reasoning, KN = Knowledge, QR = Quantitative Reasoning, VS = Visual-Spatial Processing, WM = Working Memory. The symbol P in the table indicates the primary cognitive abilities associated with the subtest, and the symbol S indicates secondary cognitive abilities associated with the subtest.

Table B.5 Definitions of the Cognitive Abilities Hypothesized as Processes Underlying SB5 Subtest Performance Listed in Table B.4

Ability	Definition
	Information Processing
Visualization of Abstract Stimuli	To apprehend the significance of pictures, drawings, or illustrations showing abstract designs and objects (e.g., geometric shapes)
Visualization of Meaningful Stimuli	To apprehend the significance of pictures, drawings, or illustrations showing lifelike scenes of people, places, and common objects
Inspection of Objects by Touch	To manually inspect with fingers and hands various objects, toys, puzzle pieces, and the like for purposes of identifying or studying them
Attention to Verbal cues	To direct one's attention to and listen for the meaning of verbal directions, clues, announcements, instructions, and so on
Attention to Visual cues	To direct one's attention to and search visually for the meaning of pictures, drawings, illustrations, objects, and the like
Impulse control	To mentally monitor movements, speech, and other responses so that emotional reactions or internal needs do not control one's actions; to delay gratification and control the timing of responses
Concentration for Long periods	To exercise mental control over one's own mental processes to examine, inspect, complete, or respond to tasks presented in the environment
Freedom from Distractibility	To screen out and avoid distracting stimuli, noise, or external demands so tasks can be completed without interruption; focused attention

(continued)

Table B.5 Continued

Ability	Definition
Freedom from Visual Neglect	To be free of the neuropsychological condition (perhaps originating in brain dysfunction) in which portions of the visual field (e.g., lower right quadrant) are blocked from perception by the examinee, the effect of the condition being that the examinee cannot see part of a picture
Toleration of Ambiguity	To show patience with difficult, ambiguous tasks, and to persevere in solving problems even when full information is unavailable
Patience with Difficult Tasks	To show patience with difficult tasks and complex problems requiring concentrated effort and perseverance in finding solutions
Speed of Movement	To quickly and rapidly move objects or one's own body to respond and complete tasks rapidly
Precision of Movement	To make precise movements with fingers, hands, and other parts of one's body to perform tasks and complete difficult duties in an accurate and effective manner
Systematic Visual Scanning	To exert control over one's eye-scanning behavior to systematically inspect a visual field, picture, illustration, written text, or other visual material prior to responding to the visual material
Wide Auditory Attention Span	To listen carefully to long sequences of sounds (speech, music, other media messages, etc.) to study them and respond to tasks required by the messages

Problem Solving

Ability	Definition
Search Strategies	To exert mental control over one's plans and actions for inspecting visual material or any visual field; to search a visual field by using an efficient plan and to effectively find important information

Table B.5 Continued

Ability	Definition
Mental Review of Potential Answers	To develop and follow a plan to examine a range of possible responses to a question, problem, or task, and to mentally scan all probable correct answers to increase chances of correctly responding and eliminating improbably wrong answers
Relating Verbal Parts to Whole	To comprehend parts of vocal speech or printed communications in relationship to the main ideas within the entire message or text
Visual Discrimination	To make fine distinctions among elements of a visual field; to identify matching or differentiated elements of the visual field
Tracking Visual Sequences	To control one's visual perception so that an entire sequence of pictures or visual events is scanned, held in memory, and then mentally reviewed and evaluated
Pattern Recognition	To apprehend visual or verbal patterns such as repeated occurrences of objects or words, and to identify repeated elements or patterns
Mental Verbal Mediation	To "talk to oneself" subvocally while attempting to solve problems or complete tasks; to employ verbal codes, memory prompts, or identifiers to assist in remembering a string of information
Fund of General Information	To accumulate general information about world events, history, scientific and literary facts, practical knowledge of how things work, and information required for daily living and to access that information
Knowledge of Culturally Relevant Facts	To be so aware and observant of facts and events in one's home or host culture that important information relevant to one's daily functioning in that culture is available; to understand the subtleties of a culture and its language, values, history, and expectations

(continued)

Table B.5 Continued

Ability	Definition
Abstract Verbal Concepts	To comprehend the subtle meanings behind printed or spoken messages and to generalize, predict, or construct inferences to additional meanings
Verbal Fluency	To speak or write in a rapid or smoothly consistent manner, recalling words at will and producing long strings of verbal explanation easily
Rapid Retrieval of Words and Explanations	To recall words, facts, concepts, and principles quickly and be able to explain their meanings; to rapidly remember verbal facts and literary meanings
Planning Ability	To reflect on tasks prior to acting on them; to use mental strategies to effectively and efficiently solve problems or achieve objectives
Trial-and-Error Strategies	To experiment (often only mentally) with different options, alternatives, or solutions to tasks to predict which option will lead to a correct solution and which alternative may lead to error
Synthesis of Information	To perceive and understand each part of a visual field or a collection of information presented in various media and to identify major themes or main ideas and integrate them into a summarizing or conclusive whole
Reproduction of Models	To study the aspects of a visual or pictorial model presented in full view and to create a replica of that model in accurate detail and composition
Cognitive Flexibility	To allow one's mind to reflect on situations and tasks and to consider a wide range of possible responses (even those that defy accepted opinions) in order to find a creative task solution
Retention Span	To use the full capacity of one's short-term and long-term memory so that great amounts of information can be stored and processed for later use

Table B.5 Continued

Ability	Definition
Visualization of Whole from Parts	To step back and view all parts of a visual field and synthesize the parts into a meaningful whole or general pattern, rather than being distracted by the attentions of individual parts or segments
Recognition and Evaluation of Pictures	To visually recognize elements of pictures, comprehend the overall meaning of illustrations, and use judgment to evaluate the purpose, message, or significance of the picture; to judge the quality of pictures
Production of Conventional Answers	To use convergent thought patterns, stored knowledge, and conventional thinking patterns to derive the typical answers to questions that most members of a population would derive; to resist the need to be unconventional when a task requires a conventional solution
Production of Creative Answers	To use reflection, planning, cognitive flexibility, and synthesis to derive new and unusual responses to questions or tasks; to make a correct but uniquely interesting response that demonstrates higher-level thinking

Appendix C

Suggested Areas of Qualitative Interpretation for the SB5

Table C.1 Possible Qualitative Interpretation Strategies for each SB5 Subtest

Item Book and Subtest	Possible Qualitative Interpretations
Item Book 1: Routing	
Nonverbal Fluid Reasoning (Object Series/Matrices)	After the stop rule is reached and SB5 testing is completed, test the examinee's ability to solve the difficult items by providing partial cues. For example, teach the examinee some strategies for solving matrices and then observe him or her making new attempts to solve the items. Have the examinee explain how he or she arrives at the answers.
Verbal Knowledge (Vocabulary)	Examine error patterns on certain types of words (e.g., noun or modifier; number of syllables; levels of word familiarity in examinee's environment or schooling). After SB5 testing is complete, test the examinee's limits by using a word in a sentence to cue a response that could stimulate memory of the meanings of words, or by asking questions about notable mistakes in a definition. Create multiple-choice vocabulary items for elderly neuropsychological patients.
Item Book 2: Nonverbal Section	
Nonverbal Knowledge	Examine error patterns in Picture Absurdities by categories such as geography, urban versus rural themes, knowledge of scientific laws of nature, or visualization ability. Prompt the examinee to scan each picture carefully before responding.

Table C.1 Continued

Item Book and Subtest	Possible Qualitative Interpretations
Nonverbal Quantitative Reasoning	Examine error patterns by curriculum areas such as number concepts, estimation, measurement, problem solving, or functional relationships. After SB5 testing is complete, test the examinee's limits by providing partial cues, expanding time limits, or emphasizing attention to certain details or numbers.
Nonverbal Visual-Spatial Processing	After SB5 testing is complete, test the examinee's limits by physically assisting in moving of the pieces while the examinee directs your movements or by providing clues to critical pieces needed in one of the Form Pattern designs.
Nonverbal Working Memory	Conduct a second testing to see if practice improves performance. After SB5 testing is complete, test the examinee's limits by presenting block taps in more exaggerated fashion and with more effort to focus attention of examinee, perhaps with use of tangible rewards such as snacks.

Item Book 3: Verbal Section

Verbal Fluid Reasoning	After SB5 testing is complete, test the examinee's limits at the lower levels by cueing examinee to the actions in the pictures at level 2, or to the importance of finding functional categories (not just colors) among the chips at level 3. On the sorting of chips, note the strategies and the examinee's sequence of category choice. At the upper levels, test the examinee's limits by providing partial clues on the Verbal Absurdities or Verbal Analogies activities.
Verbal Quantitative Reasoning	Analyze error patterns across curriculum areas. After SB5 testing is complete, test the examinee's limits by providing cues, allowing paper and pencil at earlier levels, and so on.

(continued)

Table C.1 Continued

Item Book and Subtest	Possible Qualitative Interpretations
Verbal Visual-Spatial Processing	After SB5 testing is complete, test the examinee's limits by allowing an examinee with limited communication skills to signal directions rather than vocalizing them on defining words such as *farthest* on level 3 or 4.
Working Memory	After SB5 testing is complete, test the examinee's limits by repeating questions for the elderly or hard of hearing or by allowing responses to Last Word after every two questions to study the true duration of the examinee's memory storage.

Other Sources

Test Session Behavior	After SB5 testing is complete, ask the examinee or caregiver about any unusual behavior you observed. For an examinee with hyperactivity, explore performance with and without medication, which would obviously require at least two testing sessions.

References

Aaron, P. G. (1997). The impending demise of the discrepancy formula. *Review of Educational Research, 67,* 461–502.

Achenbach, T. M. (2000). *Achenbach System of Empirically Based Assessment.* Burlington, VT: ASEBA.

Aldenderfer, M. S., & Blashfield, R. K. (1984). *Cluster analysis.* Newbury Park, CA: Sage.

American Educational Research Association, American Psychological Association, & National Council on Measurement in Education (AERA, APA, & NCME) (1999). *Standards for educational and psychological testing.* Washington, DC: American Educational Research Association.

American Psychiatric Association. (2000). *Diagnostic and statistical manual of mental disorders* (4th ed., Text Rev.). Washington, DC: Author.

American Psychological Association. (2002). Ethical principles of psychologists and code of conduct. *American Psychologist, 57,* 1060–1073.

Baddeley, A. D. (1986). *Working memory.* Oxford: Clarendon Press.

Barkley, R. A. (1990). *Attention deficit hyperactivity disorder: A handbook for diagnosis and treatment.* New York: Guilford Press.

Berk, R. A. (Ed.). (1984). *A guide to criterion-referenced test construction.* Baltimore, MD: Johns Hopkins University Press.

Binet, A., & Henri, V. (1895). La psychologie individuelle [Individual psychology]. *L'Année psychologique, 2,* 411–465.

Binet, A., & Simon, T. (1905). Méthodes nouvelles pour le diagnostic du niveau intellectual des anormaux [New methods for the diagnosis of the intellectual level of abnormals]. *L'Année psychologique, 11,* 191–336.

Binet, A., & Simon, T. (1908). Le dévelopment de l'intelligence chez les enfants [The development of intelligence in children]. *L'Année psychologique, 14,* 1–94.

Binet, A., & Simon, T. (1916). *The development of intelligence in children* (Elizabeth Kite, Trans.). Baltimore, MD: Williams & Wilkins.

Bracken, B. A., & McCallum, R. S. (1998). *The Universal Nonverbal Intelligence Test.* Itasca, IL: Riverside.

Braden, J. P. (1987). A comparison of regression and standard score methods of learning disabilities identification: Effect on racial representation. *Journal of School Psychology, 25,* 23–29.

Braden, J. P., & Elliott, S. N. (2003). *Accommodations on the Stanford-Binet Intelligence Scale, Fifth Edition* (Assessment Service Bulletin No. 2). Itasca, IL: Riverside.

Braden, J. P., & Weiss, L. (1988). Effects of simple difference versus regression discrepancy methods: An empirical study. *Journal of School Psychology, 26,* 133–142.

Carroll, J. B. (1993). *Human cognitive abilities: A survey of factor-analytic studies.* Cambridge: Cambridge University Press.

Cattell, R. B. (1943). The measurement of intelligence. *Psychological Bulletin, 40,* 153–193.

Cohen, R. J., & Swerdlik, M. E. (1999). *Psychological testing and assessment* (4th ed.). Mountain View, CA: Mayfield.

College Entrance Examination Board. (2003). *Scholastic Aptitude Tests.* Princeton, NJ: Educational Testing Service.

Conners, C. K. (1997). *Conners Rating Scales—Revised.* North Tonawanda, NY: Multi-Health Systems.

Dana, R. H. (1993). *Multicultural assessment perspectives for professional psychology.* Boston: Allyn & Bacon.

Daneman, M., & Carpenter, P. A. (1980). Individual differences in working memory and reading. *Journal of Verbal Learning and Verbal Behavior, 19,* 450–466.

Davis, F. B. (1959). Interpretation of differences among averages and individual test scores. *Journal of Educational Psychology, 50,* 162–170.

Donders, J. (1997). Sensitivity of the WISC-III to injury severity in children with traumatic head injury. *Assessment, 4,* 107–109.

Douglas, V. I. (1983). Attentional and cognitive problems. In M. Rutter (Ed.), *Developmental neuropsychiatry* (pp. 280–329). New York: Guilford Press.

Dudek, F. J. (1979). The continuing misinterpretation of the standard error of measurement. *Psychological Bulletin, 86,* 335–337.

Evans, J. J., Floyd, R. G., McGrew, K. S., & Leforgee, M. H. (2001). The relations between measures of Cattell-Horn-Carroll (CHC) cognitive abilities and reading achievement during childhood and adolescence. *School Psychology Review, 31*(2), 246–262.

Felton, R. H., & Pepper, P. P. (1995). Early identification and intervention of phonological deficits in kindergarten and early elementary children at risk for reading disability. *School Psychology Review, 24,* 405–414.

Feuerstein, R., Rand, Y., & Hoffman, M. D. (1979). *The dynamic assessment of retarded performers: The Learning Potential Assessment Device.* Baltimore, MD: University Park Press.

Flanagan, D. P., & Ortiz, S. O. (2001). *Essentials of cross-battery assessment.* New York: Wiley.

Galton, F. (1883). *Inquiries into human faculty and its development*. London: Macmillan.

Goddard, H. H. (1908). The Binet and Simon tests of intellectual capacity. *The Training School, 5,* 3–9.

Goddard, H. H. (1910). A measuring scale for intelligence. *The Training School, 6,* 146–155.

Goldman, L. S., Genel, M., Bezman, R. J., & Slanetz, P. J. (1998). Diagnosis and treatment of Attention-Deficit/Hyperactivity Disorder in children and adolescents: Council on Scientific Affairs, American Medical Association. *Journal of the American Medical Association, 279*(14), 1100–1107.

Goleman, D. (1995). *Emotional intelligence*. New York: Bantam.

Gregory, R. J. (1996). *Psychological testing* (2nd ed.). Boston: Allyn & Bacon.

Gupta, R., & Yick, A. G. (2001). Preliminary validation of the Acculturation Scale on Chinese Americans. *Journal of Social Work Research and Evaluation, 2*(1), 43–56.

Gustafsson, J. E. (1984). A unifying model for the structure of intellectual abilities. *Intelligence, 8,* 179–203.

Hess, A. K., & Weiner, I. B. (1999). *The handbook of forensic psychology* (2nd ed.). Odessa, FL: Psychological Assessment Resources.

Holland, P. W., & Thayer, D. T. (1988). Differential item performance and the Mantel-Haenszel procedure. In H. Wainer & H. Braun (Eds.), *Test validity* (pp. 129–145). Mahwah, NJ: Erlbaum.

Holland, P. W., & Wainer, H. (Eds.). (1993). *Differential item functioning*. Mahwah, NJ: Erlbaum.

Horn, J. L. (1965). *Fluid and crystallized intelligence*. Unpublished doctoral dissertation, University of Illinois, Urbana-Champaign.

Horn, J. L. (1994). Theory of fluid and crystallized intelligence. In R. J. Strenberg (Ed.), *Encyclopedia of human intelligence* (pp. 443–451). New York: Macmillan.

Horn, J. L., & Cattell, R. B. (1966). Refinement and test of the theory of fluid and crystallized general intelligences. *Journal of Educational Psychology, 57,* 253–270.

Individuals with Disabilities Education Act. (1997). 20 U.S.C. 1400 et seq: *U.S. Statutes at Large, 104,* 1103–1151.

Johnson, R. C., McClearn, G. E., Yuen, S., Nagoshi, C. T., Ahern, F. M., & Cole, R. E. (1985). Galton's data a century later. *American Psychologist, 40,* 875–892.

Joreskog, K. G., & Sorbom, D. (1999). *LISREL 8: User's reference guide*. Chicago: Scientific Software.

Kamphaus, R. W. (1993). *Clinical assessment of children's intelligence*. Boston: Allyn & Bacon.

Kamphaus, R. W. (2001). *Clinical assessment of child and adolescent intelligence* (2nd ed.). Boston: Allyn & Bacon.

Kaufman, A. S. (1990). *Assessing adolescent and adult intelligence.* Boston: Allyn & Bacon.

Kaufman, A. S. (1994). *Intelligent testing with the WISC-III.* New York: Wiley.

Kaufman, A. S., & Lichtenberger, E. O. (1999). *Essentials of WAIS-III assessment.* New York: Wiley.

Kavale, K. A., & Forness, S. R. (1995). *The nature of learning disabilities: Critical elements of diagnosis and classification.* Mahwah, NJ: Erlbaum.

Kay, K. (Ed.). (2000). *Uniquely gifted: Identifying and meeting the needs of twice-exceptional children.* Gilsum, NH: Avocus.

Ladrine, H., & Klonoff, E. A. (1994). The African American Acculturation Scale: Development, reliability, and validity. *Journal of Black Psychology, 20,* 104–127.

Lezak, M. D. (1995). *Neuropsychological assessment* (3rd ed.). New York: Oxford University Press.

Mantel, N., & Haenszel, W. (1959). Statistical aspects of the analysis of data from retrospective studies of disease. *Journal of the National Cancer Institute, 22,* 719–748.

Marin, G. (1992). Issues in the measurement of acculturation among Hispanics. In H. F. Geisinger (Ed.), Psychological testing of Hispanics (pp. 235–251). Washington, DC: American.

Marin, G., & Gamba, R. J. (1996). A new measurement of acculturation for Hispanics: The Bidimensional Acculturation Scale for Hispanics (BAS). *Hispanic Journal of Behavioral Sciences, 18,* 297–316.

McDermott, P. A., Fantuzzo, J. W., & Glutting, J. J. (1990). Just say no to subtest analysis: A critique on Wechsler theory and practice. *Journal of Psychoeducational Assessment, 8,* 290–302.

McGrew, K. S., & Flanagan, D. P. (1998). *The intelligence test desk reference (ITDR): Cf-Gc cross battery assessment.* Boston: Allyn & Bacon.

McGrew, K. S., Flanagan, D. P., Keith, T. Z., & Vanderwood, M. (1997). Beyond g: The impact of Gf-Gc specific abilities research on the future use and interpretation of intelligence test batteries in schools. *School Psychology Review, 26,* 189–210.

McGrew, K. S., & Woodcock, R. W. (2001). *Woodcock-Johnson III: Technical manual.* Itasca, IL: Riverside Publishing.

Millon, T., Millon, C., & Davis, R. (1994). *Millon Clinical Multiaxial Inventory, Third Edition.* Bloomington, MN: Pearson Assessments.

Nguyen, H. H., & von Eye, A. (2002). The Acculturation Scale for Vietnamese Adolescents (ASVA): A bidimensional perspective. *International Journal of Behavioral Development, 26,* 202–213.

Paniagua, F. A. (1994). *Assessing and treating culturally diverse clients: A practical guide.* Thousand Oaks, CA: Sage.

Pomplun, M. (2003). *The importance of working memory in the prediction of achievement.* Itasca, IL: Riverside Publishing.

President's Commission on Excellence in Special Education. (2002). *A new era: Revitalizing special education for children and their families.* Washington, DC: U.S. Department of Education.

Rasch, G. (1980). *Probabilistic models for some intelligence and attainment tests.* Chicago: University of Chicago Press.

Riverside Publishing. (2003). *SB5 training materials* [PowerPoint presentation]. Itasca, IL: Author.

Roid, G. H. (1994). Patterns of writing skills derived from cluster analysis of direct-writing assessments. *Applied Measurement in Education, 7*(2), 159–170.

Roid, G. H. (2003a). *Development of enhanced composite scores for clinical interpretation.* Technical supplement for the Stanford-Binet Intelligence Scales—Fifth Edition. Itasca, IL: Riverside Publishing.

Roid, G. H. (2003b). *Stanford-Binet Intelligence Scales–Fifth Edition.* Itasca, IL: Riverside Publishing.

Roid, G. H. (2003c). *Stanford-Binet Intelligence Scales–Fifth Edition: Examiner's manual.* Itasca, IL: Riverside Publishing.

Roid, G. H. (2003d). *Stanford-Binet Intelligence Scales–Fifth Edition: Interpretive manual.* Itasca, IL: Riverside Publishing.

Roid, G. H. (2003e). *Stanford-Binet Intelligence Scales–Fifth Edition: Scoring Pro* [Computer software]. Itasca, IL: Riverside Publishing.

Roid, G. H. (2003f). *Stanford-Binet Intelligence Scales–Fifth Edition: Technical manual.* Itasca, IL: Riverside Publishing.

Roid, G. H., & Gyurke, J. (1991). General-factor and specific variance in the WPPSI-R. *Journal of Psychoeducational Assessment, 9,* 209–223.

Roid, G. H., & Miller, L. J. (1997). *Leiter International Performance Scale—Revised.* Wood Dale, IL: Stoelting.

Roid, G. H., Prifitera, A., & Weiss, L. G. (1993). Replication of the WISC-III factor structure in an independent sample. In B. A. Bracken & R. S. McCallum (Eds.), *Journal of Psychoeducational Assessment monograph series, Advances in assessment: Wechsler Intelligence Scale for Children—Third Edition* (pp. 6–21). Germantown, TN: Psychoeducational Corporation.

Roid, G. H., & Pomplun, M. (2004). *The Stanford-Binet Fifth Edition.* In D. Flanagan & P. Harrison (Eds.), *Contemporary intellectual assessment* (2nd ed., chap. 17). New York: Guilford Press.

Ross, R. P. (1995). Impact on psychologists of state guidelines for evaluating under achievement. *Learning Disabilities Quarterly, 18*(1), 43–56.

Ryan, J. J., Lamarche, J. A., Barth, J. T., & Boll, T. J. (1996). Neuropsychological consequences and treatment of pediatric head trauma. In L. S. Batchelor &

R. S. Dean (Eds.), *Pediatric neuropsychology* (pp. 117–137). Needham Heights, MA: Allyn & Bacon.

Salovey, P., & Mayer, J. D. (1990). Emotional intelligence. *Imagination, Cognition, and Personality, 9,* 185–211.

Sattler, J. M. (1988). *Assessment of children* (3rd ed.). San Diego, CA: Author.

Sattler, J. M. (2002). *Assessment of children* (4th ed.). San Diego, CA: Author.

Schwean, V. L., & Saklofske, D. H. (1998). WISC-III assessment of children with Attention-Deficit/Hyperactivity Disorder. In A. Prifitera & D. Saklofske (Eds.), *WISC-III: Clinical use and interpretation* (pp. 91–118). San Diego, CA: Academic Press.

Shepard, L. A. (1980). An evaluation of the regression discrepancy method for identifying children with learning disabilities. *Journal of Special Education, 14,* 79–91.

Silverstein, A. B. (1982). Pattern analysis as simultaneous statistical inference. *Journal of Consulting and Clinical Psychology, 50,* 234–240.

Snowden, L. R., & Hines, A. M. (1999). A scale to assess African American acculturation. *Journal of Black Psychology, 25,* 36–47.

Stern, W. (1914). *The psychological methods of testing intelligence.* Baltimore, MD: Warwick & York.

Stuebing, K. K., Fletcher, J. M., LeDoux, J. M., Lyon, G. R., Shaywitz, S. E., & Shaywitz, B. A. (2002). Validity of IQ-discrepancy classifications of reading disabilities: A meta-analysis. *American Educational Research Journal, 39,* 469–518.

Szatmari, P. (1992). The epidemiology of Attention-Deficit/Hyperactivity Disorders. In G. Weiss (Ed.), *Child and adolescent psychiatry clinics of North America: Attention Deficit Disorder* (pp. 361–372). Philadelphia, PA: W. B. Saunders.

Taylor, R. L. (2003). *Assessment of exceptional students* (6th ed.). Boston, MA: Allyn & Bacon.

Tellegen, A., & Briggs, P. F. (1967). Old wine in new skins: Grouping Wechsler subtests into new scales. *Journal of Consulting Psychology, 31,* 499–506.

Terman, L. M. (1911). The Binet-Simon Scale for measuring intelligence: Impressions gained by its application. *Psychological Clinic, 5,* 199–206.

Terman, L. M. (1916). *The measurement of intelligence: An explanation of and a complete guide for the use of the Stanford revision and extension of the Binet-Simon Scale.* Boston: Houghton Mifflin.

Terman, L. M., & Child, H. G. (1912). A tentative revision and extension of the Binet-Simon Measuring Scale of Intelligence. *Journal of Educational Psychology, 3,* 61–74, 133–143, 198–208, 277–289.

Terman, L. M., & Merrill, M. A. (1937). *Measuring intelligence.* Boston: Houghton Mifflin.

Terman, L. M., & Merrill, M. A. (1960). *Stanford-Binet Intelligence Scale: Manual for the Third Revision Form L-M.* Boston: Houghton Mifflin.

Terman, L. M., & Merrill, M. A. (1973). *Stanford-Binet Intelligence Scale: Manual for the Third Revision Form L-M, 1973 norms edition.* Boston: Houghton Mifflin.

Thorndike, R. L., & Hagen, E. P. (1994). *Cognitive Abilities Test* (2nd ed.). Itasca, IL: Riverside Publishing.

Thorndike, R. L., Hagen, E. P., & Sattler, J. M. (1986). *The Stanford-Binet Intelligence Scale: Fourth Edition guide for administering and scoring.* Itasca, IL: Riverside Publishing.

Thurlow, M. L., Elliott, J. L., & Ysseldyke, J. E. (1998). *Testing students with disabilities: Practical strategies for complying with district and state requirements.* Thousand Oaks, CA: Corwin Press.

Torgesen, J. K. (2002). The prevention of reading difficulties. *Journal of School Psychology, 40,* 7–26.

U.S. Census Bureau (2001). *Census 2000 Summary File 1 United States.* Washington, DC: Author.

Wainer, H. (Ed.). (1990). *Computerized adaptive testing: A primer.* Hillsdale, NJ: Erlbaum.

Wechsler, D. (1991). *Wechsler Intelligence Scale for Children—Third Edition.* San Antonio, TX: The Psychological Corporation.

Wechsler, D. (1997). *Wechsler Adult Intelligence Scale—Third Edition.* San Antonio, TX: The Psychological Corporation.

Wechsler, D. (2003). *Wechsler Intelligence Scale for Children—Fourth Edition.* San Antonio, TX: The Psychological Corporation.

Weiss, M., Murray, C., Weiss, G. (2002). Adults with Attention-Deficit/Hyperactivity Disorder: Current concepts. *Journal of Psychiatric Practice, 8,* 46–55.

Wilson, K. M., & Swanson, H. L. (2001). Are mathematics disabilities due to a domain-general or a domain-specific working memory deficit? *Journal of Learning Disabilities, 34*(3), 237–248.

Wolf, T. H. (1969). The emergence of Binet's conceptions and measurement of intelligence: A case history of the creative process. Part II. *Journal of the History of the Behavioral Sciences, 5,* 207–237.

Wolf, T. H. (1973). *Alfred Binet.* Chicago: University of Chicago Press.

Woodcock, R. W. (1999). What can Rasch-based scores convey about a person's test performance? In S. E. Embretson & S. L. Hershberger (Eds.), *The new rules of measurement: What every psychologist and educator should know* (pp. 105–128). Mahwah, NJ: Erlbaum.

Woodcock, R. W., & Dahl, M. N. (1971). *A common scale for the measurement of person ability and test item difficulty.* (AGS Paper No. 10). Circle Pines, MN: American Guidance Service.

Woodcock, R. W., McGrew, K. S., & Mather, N. (2001a). *Woodcock-Johnson III Tests of Achievement.* Itasca, IL: Riverside Publishing.

Woodcock, R. W., McGrew, K. S., & Mather, N. (2001b). *Woodcock-Johnson III Tests of Cognitive Abilities.* Itasca, IL: Riverside Publishing.

Wright & Lineacre. (1999). *WINSTEPS: Rasch analysis for all two-facet models.* Chicago: MESA Press.

Annotated Bibliography

American Educational Research Association, American Psychological Association, & National Council on Measurement in Education. (1999). *Standards for educational and psychological testing.* Washington, DC: APA.

This important book presents the official standards for test developers, examiners, and consumers, including guidelines for development procedures, technical qualities, publication characteristics, examiner and consumer responsibilities, and much more.

American Psychiatric Association. (2000). *Diagnostic and statistical manual of mental disorders* (4th ed., Text Rev.). Washington, DC: Author

As discussed in Chapters 4 and 6, diagnoses of psychological and psychiatric conditions are typically based on the DSM-IV-TR criteria, and not solely on test results. Examiners using SB5 for diagnoses should be thoroughly familiar with this current version of an important reference.

American Psychological Association. (2002). Ethical principles of psychologists and code of conduct. *American Psychologist, 57,* 1060–1073.

The standard reference for ethical concerns in psychological testing.

Binet, A., & Simon, T. (1916). *The development of intelligence in children* (Elizabeth Kite, Trans.). Baltimore, MD: Williams & Wilkins.

Students interested in the history of assessment (and the history of psychology as a whole) would find this translation of the original Binet-Simon scales very interesting.

Carroll, J. B. (1993). *Human cognitive abilities: A survey of factor-analytic studies.* Cambridge; New York: Cambridge University Press.

The definitive research report on cognitive factors and the hierarchical g models such as CHC theory. Defines and gives many examples of reasoning, knowledge (language), visual, and memory factors and instruments to measure them.

Dana, R. H. (1993). *Multicultural assessment perspectives for professional psychology.* Boston: Allyn & Bacon; *or* Paniagua, F. A. (1994). *Assessing and treating culturally diverse clients: A practical guide.* Thousand Oaks, CA: Sage.

Two important books for examiners who wish to understand and measure acculturation and understand assessment issues for culturally diverse clients.

Flanagan, D. P., & Ortiz, S. O. (2001). *Essentials of cross-battery assessment.* New York: Wiley; *or* McGrew, K. S., & Flanagan, D. P. (1998). *The intelligence test desk reference (ITDR): Gf-Gc cross battery assessment.* Boston: Allyn & Bacon.

Two important books that define the cross-battery assessment method and that would enhance interpretation of the SB5 because of its basis in CHC theory (formerly known as Gf-Gc or fluid-crystallized theory).

Gregory, R. J. (1996). *Psychological testing* (2nd ed.). Boston: Allyn & Bacon; *or* Kamphaus, R. W. (2001). *Clinical assessment of child and adolescent intelligence* (2nd ed.). Boston: Allyn & Bacon; *or* Taylor, R. L. (2003). *Assessment of exceptional students* (6th ed.). Boston: Allyn & Bacon.

Three useful textbooks from Allyn and Bacon publishers for students of assessment, covering psychometric methods and surveys of tests in several domains of usage.

Hess, A. K., & Weiner, I. B. (1999). *The handbook of forensic psychology* (2nd ed.). Odessa, FL: Psychological Assessment Resources.

A key reference for situations in which SB5 results may be used in legal, law-enforcement, judicial, or correctional settings.

Lezak, M. D. (1995). *Neuropsychological assessment* (3rd ed.). New York: Oxford University Press.

The definitive book on neuropsychological assessment, including theory, research, and a multitude of instruments. An important type of reference for understanding learning disabilities, Attention-Deficit/Hyperactivity Disorder, and other cognitive-process deficits.

McGrew, K. S., & Woodcock, R. W. (2001). *Woodcock-Johnson III: Technical manual.* Itasca, IL: Riverside Publishing.

Another source of information on the methods used to develop SB5 change-sensitive scores (CSS). The CSS and Rasch item-response-theory methods are used in the W-scores of WJ III.

President's Commission on Excellence in Special Education. (2002). *A new era: Revitalizing special education for children and their families.* Washington, DC: U.S. Department of Education.

Important reference showing the emerging trends in special education assessment. Use of SB5 scores may change depending on the final outcome of Individuals With Disabilities Education Act reauthorization and legal implementation in each state of the federal laws regarding qualification for special-education services and funding.

Roid, G. H. (2003). *Stanford-Binet Intelligence Scales—Fifth Edition: Examiner's manual, Interpretive manual, Scoring Pro [software], and Technical manual.* Itasca, IL: Riverside Publishing.

The official resources for SB5 norms and details of development, standardization, technical qualities, and so on.

Sattler, J. M. (2002). *Assessment of children* (4th ed.). San Diego, CA: Author.

Another important book on assessment by one of the authors of the Stanford-Binet Fourth Edition. Provides a number of key tables and references.

Thurlow, M. L., Elliott, J. L., & Ysseldyke, J. E. (1998). *Testing students with disabilities: Practical strategies for complying with district and state requirements.* Thousand Oaks, CA: Corwin Press.

A good resource for implementing accommodations in assessment.

Woodcock, R. W. (1999). What can Rasch-based scores convey about a person's test performance? In S. E. Embretson & S. L. Hershberger (Eds.), *The new rules of measurement: What every psychologist and educator should know* (pp. 105–128). Mahwah, NJ: Erlbaum.

For users of SB5 CSS scores, Woodcock presents fundamental concepts of using Rasch-based scores. Written from the perspective of the Woodcock-Johnson tests, but useful for understanding CSS scores. Also, the book by Embretson and Hershberger gives the important principles of the new item-response-theory approach to measurement, which will become more and more prominent in the future.

Index

ABIQ. *See* Abbreviated Battery IQ
Abbreviated Battery IQ, 3, 50, 59
Absurdities. *See* Activities
Accommodations, 20, 24–27, 69–
    70
  access skills, 26
  target skills, 26
Acculturation, 70–71
Activities, 30–50, 170–173
  Block Span, 42, 46
  Delayed Response, 39
  Early Reasoning, 45–46
  Form Board, 39
  Form Patterns, 39–41
  Last Word, 49–50
  Object-Series/Matrices, 30–32,
    170
  Picture Absurdities, 3, 9, 105–10,
    110
  Procedural Knowledge, 36–37
  Position and Direction, 49
  Quantitative Reasoning, 37–38,
    48–49
  Vocabulary, 1, 9, 32, 134
  Verbal Absurdities, 47–48
  Verbal Analogies, 47–48
ADHD. *See* Attention Deficit
  Hyperactivity Disorder

Administration:
  accommodating (*see*
    Accommodations)
  administration time, 16
  assumptions (*see* Interpretation)
  basal and ceiling, 34–35
  definition of terms, 21
  examiner tips, 33, 37–38, 43–44
  item books, 27–29, 30, 33, 44,
    182–184
  modifications, 25
  plastic tray, 21
  presentation format, 26
  prompt rule, 32
  rapport, 22–23
  response format, 26
  reverse rule, 29
  standard order of, 27–28
  start point, 25, 29
  starting and stopping rules, 29
  teaching items, 30
  testlets, 21, 34–35
  timing, 16, 26
Age equivalents, 59, 62–63
Applications, clinical
  ADHD (*see* Attention Deficit
    Hyperactivity Disorder)
  forensic, 131–133

About the Authors

Gale H. Roid, PhD, is currently Visiting Scholar, Simpson College and Graduate School in California. He was previously Dunn Professor of Educational and Psychological Assessment, Peabody College of Vanderbilt University. He is author of the Stanford-Binet Intelligence Scale—Fifth Edition (2003) and senior author of the Leiter International Performance Scale—Revised Edition (1997). He was formerly professor of psychology, George Fox University, Graduate School of Clinical Psychology (1993–1999). He was senior project director for The Psychological Corporation, where he was the initial project director for the Wechsler Intelligence Scale for Children—Third Edition (WISC-III) and related tests (WIAT and WAIS-III) from 1987 to 1992. He was previously a technical consultant to the Oregon Statewide Assessment Program, 1985–1997; director of research for the test publisher Western Psychological Services in Los Angeles, 1980–1985; research professor, Teaching Research Division of the Oregon State System of Higher Education, 1972–1979; and an assistant professor of psychology, McGill University, Montreal, Canada, 1969–1972.

Dr. Roid earned an A.B. from Harvard University in 1965 and his PhD in psychological assessment from the University of Oregon in 1969. He is the author or coauthor of 9 published tests, 3 books, 9 book chapters, more than 20 research articles in refereed journals, and more than 60 refereed convention papers. He has been a technical consultant for over 40 published tests and manuals. He is a fellow of Division 5 of the American Psychological Association, and consulting editor for the journal *Applied Measurement in Education*. He received a diplomate designation by the American Board of Assessment Psychology in 1996.

R. Andrew Barram, PsyD, is a licensed clinical psychologist in Bend, Oregon, specializing in assessment and general clinical treatment. Dr. Barram was involved in the development of the SB5 as an independent consultant from the Pilot Study phase through publication. His involvement focused on improving the person-test interface of the instrument and, later, on training examiners for the Try-Out and Standardization phases. He assisted in the development of several SB5 items and tasks and provided consultation on the clinical applications of SB5.

Dr. Barram provides psychological consultation and assessments within the forensic arena as well as for treatment facilities, physicians, and counselors. His clinical treatment services include individual counseling for adolescents and adults, as well as couples counseling. Dr. Barram has worked in a wide range of clinical settings. In the Denver, Colorado, area he provided clinical services in adolescent residential treatment programs and both Adams and Aurora County mental health centers. In the Portland, Oregon, area he provided services within an emergency room, an acute psychiatric inpatient center, a child residential treatment facility, and public schools. Dr. Barram gained forensic experience working within the Federal Correctional Institution at Sheridan, Oregon, and the Adams County Jail in Colorado. Dr. Barram volunteered with crisis response networks in Oregon and Colorado. Dr. Barram also provided some assistance in the development of the Leiter International Performance Scale. He obtained his doctorate from the Graduate School of Clinical Psychology, George Fox University, in 1998.

Maeve Binchy

London Transports

Delta Trade Paperbacks

LONDON TRANSPORTS
A Delta Book

PUBLISHING HISTORY
First published in Great Britain in 1978 and 1980 by Quartet Books and Ward River
Press Limited
Dell mass market edition published June 1995
Delta Trade Paperback edition / June 2007

Published by
Bantam Dell
A Division of Random House, Inc.
New York, New York

"Warren Street" was first published as "The Dressmaker's Dilemma" in *Woman's Own,*
June 1979; "Victoria" and "Pimlico" were first published in *The Irish Times,* 1979;
"Euston" was first published as "Forgiveness" in *The Irish Times,* 1982.

Charing Cross Bridge (1906) by Andre Derain / Musée d'Orsay, Paris, copyright ©
SuperStock, Inc. / SuperStock

ISBN 978-0-385-34177-6

Printed in the United States of America

www.bantamdell.com

BVG 10 9 8 7 6 5 4 3 2